OTHER PEOPLE'S MONEY

AND HOW THE BANKERS USE IT

BY

LOUIS D. BRANDEIS

NEW YORK

FREDERICK A. STOKES COMPANY

PUBLISHERS

Printed in the United States of America

OTHER PEOPLE'S MONEY

AND HOW THE BANKERS USE IT

BY
LOUIS D. BRANDEIS

Martino Publishing

Mansfield Centre, CT

2009

Martino Publishing
P.O. Box 373,
Mansfield Centre, CT 06250 USA

www.martinopublishing.com

ISBN-13: 978-1-57898-738-2 (softcover: alk. paper)
ISBN-10: 1-57898-738-5 (softcover: alk. paper)
ISBN-13: 978-1-57898-739-9 (hardcover: alk. paper)
ISBN-10: 1-57898-739-3 (hardcover: alk. paper)

© 2009 Martino Publishing

Library of Congress Cataloging-in-Publication Data

Brandeis, Louis Dembitz, 1856-1941.
  Other people's money: and how the bankers use it / by
Louis D. Brandeis.
    p. cm.
  Includes bibliographical references and index.
  Reprint. Originally published: New York: F.A. Stokes, 1914.
  ISBN-13: 978-1-57898-738-2 (softcover: alk. paper)
  ISBN-10: 1-57898-738-5 (softcover: alk. paper)
  ISBN-13: 978-1-57898-739-9 (hardcover: alk. paper)
  ISBN-10: 1-57898-739-3 (hardcover: alk. paper)
  1. Finance--United States. 2. Banks and banking--United
States. I. Title.

HG181.B8 2009
332.1'750973--dc22   2009008576

Cover design by T. Matarazzo

Printed in the United States of America On 100% Acid-Free Paper

PREFACE

W_{HILE} Louis D. Brandeis's series of articles on the money trust was running in Harper's Weekly many inquiries came about publication in more accessible permanent form. Even without such urgence through the mail, however, it would have been clear that these articles inevitably constituted a book, since they embodied an analysis and a narrative by that mind which, on the great industrial movements of our era, is the most expert in the United States. The inquiries meant that the attentive public recognized that here was a contribution to history. Here was the clearest and most profound treatment ever published on that part of our business development which, as President Wilson and other wise men have said, has come to constitute the greatest of our problems. The story of our time is the story of industry. No scholar of the future will be able to describe our era with authority unless he comprehends that expansion and concentration which followed the harnessing of steam and electricity, the great uses of the change, and the great excesses. No historian of the future, in my opinion, will find among our contemporary documents so masterful an analysis of why concentration went astray. I am but one among many who look upon Mr. Brandeis as having, in the field of economics, the most inventive and sound mind of our time. While his articles were running in Harper's Weekly I had ample opportunity to know how widespread was the belief among intelligent men that this brilliant diagnosis of our money trust was the most important contribution to current thought in many years.

"Great" is one of the words that I do not use loosely, and I look upon Mr. Brandeis as a great man. In the composition of his intellect, one of the most important elements is his comprehension of figures. As one of the leading financiers of the country said to me, "Mr. Brandeis's greatness as a lawyer is part of his greatness as a mathematician." My views on this subject are sufficiently indicated in the following editorial in Harper's Weekly.

ARITHMETIC

About five years before the Metropolitan Traction Company of New York went into the hands of a receiver, Mr. Brandeis came down from Boston, and in a speech at Cooper Union prophesied that that company must fail.

Leading bankers in New York and Boston were heartily recommending the stock to their customers. Mr. Brandeis made his prophecy merely by analyzing the published figures. How did he win in the Pinchot-Glavis-Ballinger controversy? In various ways, no doubt; but perhaps the most critical step was when he calculated just how long it would take a fast worker to go through the Glavis-Ballinger record and make a judgment of it; whereupon he decided that Mr. Wickersham could not have made his report at the time it was stated to have been made, and therefore it must have been predated.

Most of Mr. Brandeis's other contributions to current history have involved arithmetic. When he succeeded in preventing a raise in freight rates, it was through an exact analysis of cost. When he got Savings Bank Insurance started in Massachusetts, it was by being able to figure what insurance ought to cost. When he made the best contract between a city and a public utility that exists in this country, a definite grasp of the gas business was necessary—combined, of course, with the wisdom and originality that make a statesman. He could not have invented the preferential shop if that new idea had not been founded on a precise knowledge of the conditions in the garment trades. When he established before the United States Supreme Court the constitutionality of legislation affecting women only, he relied much less upon reason than upon the amount of knowledge displayed of what actually happens to women when they are overworked—which, while not arithmetic, is built on the same intellectual quality. Nearly two years before Mr. Mellen resigned from the New Haven Railroad, Mr. Brandeis wrote to the present editor of this paper a private letter in which he said:

"When the New Haven reduces its dividends and Mellen resigns, the 'Decline of New Haven and Fall of Mellen' will make a dramatic story of human interest with a moral—or two—including the evils of private monopoly. Events cannot be long deferred, and possibly you may want to prepare for their coming.

"Anticipating the future a little, I suggest the following as an epitaph or obituary notice:

"Mellen was a masterful man, resourceful, courageous, broad of view. He fired the imagination of New England; but, being oblique of vision, merely distorted its judgment and silenced its conscience. For a while he trampled with impunity on laws human and divine; but, as he was obsessed with the delusion that two and two make five, he fell, at last, a victim to the relentless rules of humble arithmetic.

"'Remember, O Stranger, Arithmetic is the first of the sciences and the mother of safety.'"

The exposure of the bad financial management of the New Haven railroad, more than any other one thing, led to the exposure and comprehension of the wasteful methods of big business all over the country and that exposure of the New Haven was the almost single-handed work of Mr. Brandeis. He is a person who fights against any odds while it is necessary to fight and stops fighting as soon as the fight is won. For a long time very respectable and honest leaders of finance said that his charges against the New Haven were unsound and inexcusable. He kept ahead. A year before the actual crash came, however, he ceased worrying, for he knew the work had been carried far enough

to complete itself. When someone asked him
to take part in some little controversy shortly
before the collapse, he replied, "That fight does
not need me any longer. Time and arithmetic
will do the rest."

This grasp of the concrete is combined in Mr.
Brandeis with an equally distinguished grasp of
bearing and significance. His imagination is as
notable as his understanding of business. In
those accomplishments which have given him his
place in American life, the two sides of his mind
have worked together. The arrangement between the Gas Company and the City of Boston
rests on one of the guiding principles of Mr.
Brandeis's life, that no contract is good that is
not advantageous to both parties to it. Behind
his understanding of the methods of obtaining
insurance and the proper cost of it to the laboring
man lay a philosophy of the vast advantage to
the fibre and energy of the community that would
come from devising methods by which the laboring classes could make themselves comfortable
through their whole lives and thus perhaps making unnecessary elaborate systems of state help.
The most important ideas put forth in the
Armstrong Committee Report on insurance had
been previously suggested by Mr. Brandeis,

acting as counsel for the Equitable policy
holders.   Business and the more important
statesmanship were intimately combined in the
management of the Protocol in New York,
which has done so much to improve conditions in the clothing industry.   The welfare
of the laborer and his relation to his employer
seems to Mr. Brandeis, as it does to all the
most competent thinkers today, to constitute
the most important question we have to solve,
and he won the case, coming up to the Supreme
Court of the United States, from Oregon, estab-
lishing the constitutionality of special protective
legislation for women.   In the Minimum Wage
case, also from the State of Oregon, which is
about to be heard before the Supreme Court, he
takes up what is really a logical sequence of the
limitation of women's hours in certain industries,
since it would be a futile performance to limit
their hours and then allow their wages to be cut
down in consequence.   These industrial activities
are in large part an expression of his deep and
ever growing sympathy with the working people
and understanding of them.   Florence Kelley
once said: "No man since Lincoln has understood
the common people as Louis Brandeis does."

While the majority of Mr. Brandeis's great progressive achievements have been connected with the industrial system, some have been political in a more limited sense. I worked with him through the Ballinger-Pinchot controversy, and I never saw a grasp of detail more brilliantly combined with high constructive ethical and political thinking. After the man who knew most about the details of the Interior Department had been cross-examined by Mr. Brandeis he came and sat down by me and said: "Mr. Hapgood, I have no respect for you. I do not think your motives in this agitation are good motives, but I want to say that you have a wonderful lawyer. He knows as much about the Interior Department today as I do." In that controversy, the power of the administration and of the ruling forces in the House and Senate were combined to protect Secretary Ballinger and prevent the truth from coming to light. Mr. Brandeis, in leading the fight or the conservation side, was constantly haunted by the idea that there was a mystery somewhere. The editorial printed above hints at how he solved the mystery, but it would require much more space to tell the other sides, the enthusiasm for conservation, the convincing arguments

for higher standards in office, the connection
of this conspiracy with the country's larger
needs. Seldom is an audience at a hearing so
moved as it was by Mr. Brandeis's final plea to
the committee.

Possibly his work on railroads will turn out to be
the most significant among the many things Mr.
Brandeis has done. His arguments in 1910–11
before the Interstate Commerce Commission
against the raising of rates, on the ground that
the way for railroads to be more prosperous was
to be more efficient, made efficiency a national
idea. It is a cardinal point in his philosophy
that the only real progress toward a higher national life will come through efficiency in all our
activities. The seventy-eight questions addressed
to the railroads by the Interstate Commerce
Commission in December, 1913, embody what
is probably the most comprehensive embodiment
of his thought on the subject.

On nothing has he ever worked harder than on
his diagnosis of the Money Trust, and when his
life comes to be written (I hope many years hence)
this will be ranked with his railroad work for
its effect in accelerating industrial changes. It
is indeed more than a coincidence that so many
of the things he has been contending for have

come to pass. It is seldom that one man puts
one idea, not to say many ideas, effectively
before the world, but it is no exaggeration to say
that Mr. Brandeis is responsible for the now widespread recognition of the inherent weakness of
great size. He was the first person who set forth
effectively the doctrine that there is a limit to the
size of greatest efficiency, and the successful demonstration of that truth is a profound contribution to the subject of trusts. The demonstration
is powerfully put in his testimony before the
Senate Committee in 1911, and it is powerfully
put in this volume. In destroying the delusion
that efficiency was a common incident of size, he
emphasized the possibility of efficiency through
intensive development of the individual, thus
connecting this principle with his whole study of
efficiency, and pointing the way to industrial
democracy.

Not less notable than the intellect and the
constructive ability that have gone into Mr.
Brandeis's work are the exceptional moral qualities. Any powerful and entirely sincere crusader
must sacrifice much. Mr. Brandeis has sacrificed
much in money, in agreeableness of social life,
in effort, and he has done it for principle and for
human happiness. His power of intensive work,

his sustained interest and will, and his courage have been necessary for leadership. No man could have done what he has done without being willing to devote his life to making his dreams come true.

Nor should anyone make the mistake, because the labors of Mr. Brandeis and others have recently brought about changes, that the system which was being attacked has been undermined. The currency bill has been passed, and as these words are written, it looks as if a group of trust bills would be passed. But systems are not ended in a day. Of the truths which are embodied in the essays printed in this book, some are being carried out now, but it will be many, many years before the whole idea can be made effective; and there will, therefore, be many, many years during which active citizens will be struggling for those principles which are here so clearly, so eloquently, so conclusively set forth.

The articles reprinted here were all written before November, 1913. "The Failure of Banker Management" appeared in Harper's Weekly Aug. 16, 1913; the other articles, between Nov. 22, 1913 and Jan. 17, 1914.

NORMAN HAPGOOD.

March, 1914.

CONTENTS

OTHER PEOPLE'S MONEY
AND HOW THE BANKERS USE IT

CHAPTER I

OUR FINANCIAL OLIGARCHY

PRESIDENT WILSON, when Governor, declared in 1911:

"The great monopoly in this country is the money monopoly. So long as that exists, our old variety and freedom and individual energy of development are out of the question. A great industrial nation is controlled by its system of credit. Our system of credit is concentrated. The growth of the nation, therefore, and all our activities are in the hands of a few men, who, even if their actions be honest and intended for the public interest, are necessarily concentrated upon the great undertakings in which their own money is involved and who, necessarily, by every reason of their own limitations, chill and check and destroy genuine economic freedom. This is the greatest question of all; and to this, states-

1

men must address themselves with an earnest determination to serve the long future and the true liberties of men."

The Pujo Committee—appointed in 1912—found:

"Far more dangerous than all that has happened to us in the past in the way of elimination of competition in industry is the control of credit through the domination of these groups over our banks and industries." . . .

"Whether under a different currency system the resources in our banks would be greater or less is comparatively immaterial if they continue to be controlled by a small group." . . .

"It is impossible that there should be competition with all the facilities for raising money or selling large issues of bonds in the hands of these few bankers and their partners and allies, who together dominate the financial policies of most of the existing systems. . . .   The acts of this inner group, as here described, have nevertheless been more destructive of competition than anything accomplished by the trusts, for they strike at the very vitals of potential competition in every industry that is under their protection, a condition which if permitted to continue, will render impossible all attempts to restore normal competitive conditions in the industrial world. . . .

"If the arteries of credit now clogged well-nigh to choking by the obstructions created through the control of these groups are opened so that they may be permitted freely to play their important part in the financial system, competition in large enterprises will become possible and business can be conducted on its merits instead of being subject to the tribute and the good will of this handful of self-constituted trustees of the national prosperity."

The promise of New Freedom was joyously proclaimed in 1913.

The facts which the Pujo Investigating Committee and its able Counsel, Mr. Samuel Untermyer, have laid before the country, show clearly the means by which a few men control the business of America. The report proposes measures which promise some relief. Additional remedies will be proposed. Congress will soon be called upon to act.

How shall the emancipation be wrought? On what lines shall we proceed? The facts, when fully understood, will teach us.

The dominant element in our financial oligarchy is the investment banker. Associated banks, trust companies and life insurance companies are his tools. Controlled railroads, public service and industrial corporations are his subjects. Though properly but middlemen, these bankers bestride as masters America's business world, so that practically no large enterprise can be undertaken successfully without their participation or approval. These bankers are, of course, able men possessed of large fortunes; but the most potent factor in their control of business is not the possession of extraordinary ability or huge wealth. The key to their power is Combination—concentration intensive and comprehensive—advancing on three distinct lines:

First: There is the obvious consolidation of banks and trust companies; the less obvious affiliations—through stockholdings, voting trusts and interlocking directorates—of banking institutions which are not legally connected; and the joint transactions, gentlemen's agreements, and "banking ethics" which eliminate competition among the investment bankers.

Second: There is the consolidation of railroads into huge systems, the large combinations of public service corporations and the formation of industrial trusts, which, by making businesses so "big" that local, independent banking concerns cannot alone supply the necessary funds, has created dependence upon the associated New York bankers.

But combination, however intensive, along these lines only, could not have produced the Money Trust—another and more potent factor of combination was added.

Third: Investment bankers, like J. P. Morgan & Co., dealers in bonds, stocks and notes, encroached upon the functions of the three other classes of corporations with which their business brought them into contact. They became the directing power in railroads, public service and industrial companies through which our great business operations are conducted—the makers of bonds and stocks. They became the directing power in the life insurance companies, and other corporate reservoirs of the people's savings—the buyers of bonds and stocks. They became the directing power also in banks and trust companies—the depositaries of the quick capital of the country—the life blood of business, with which they and others carried on their operations. Thus four distinct functions, each essential to business,

and each exercised, originally, by a distinct set of
men, became united in the investment banker.
It is to this union of business functions that the
existence of the Money Trust is mainly due.*

The development of our financial oligarchy
followed, in this respect, lines with which the
history of political despotism has familiarized us:
—usurpation, proceeding by gradual encroachment rather than by violent acts; subtle and
often long-concealed concentration of distinct
functions, which are beneficent when separately
administered, and dangerous only when combined
in the same persons. It was by processes such
as these that Cæsar Augustus became master of
Rome. The makers of our own Constitution
had in mind like dangers to our political liberty
when they provided so carefully for the separation
of governmental powers.

THE PROPER SPHERE OF THE INVESTMENT BANKER

The original function of the investment banker
was that of dealer in bonds, stocks and notes;
buying mainly at wholesale from corporations,

---

*Obviously only a few of the investment bankers exer-
cise this great power; but many others perform important functions in the system, as hereinafter described.

municipalities, states and governments which need money, and selling to those seeking investments. The banker performs, in this respect, the function of a merchant; and the function is a very useful one. Large business enterprises are conducted generally by corporations. The permanent capital of corporations is represented by bonds and stocks. The bonds and stocks of the more important corporations are owned, in large part, by small investors, who do not participate in the management of the company. Corporations require the aid of a banker-middleman, for they lack generally the reputation and clientele essential to selling their own bonds and stocks direct to the investor. Investors in corporate securities, also, require the services of a banker-middleman. The number of securities upon the market is very large. Only a part of these securities is listed on the New York Stock Exchange; but its listings alone comprise about sixteen hundred different issues aggregating about $26,500,000,000, and each year new listings are made averaging about two·hundred and thirty-three to an amount of $1,500,000,000. For a small investor to make an intelligent selection from these many corporate securities—indeed, to pass an intelligent judgment upon a single one—is ordinarily impossible. He lacks the ability, the facilities, the training and the time essential to a proper investigation. Unless his purchase is to be little better than a gamble, he needs the advice of an expert, who, combining special knowledge with judgment, has the facilities and incentive to make a thorough investigation. This dependence, both of corporations and of investors, upon the banker has grown in recent years, since women and others who do not participate in the management, have become the owners of so large a part of the stocks and bonds of our great corporations. Over half of the stockholders of the American Sugar Refining Company and nearly half of the stockholders of the Pennsylvania Railroad and of the New York, New Haven & Hartford Railroad are women.

Good-will—the possession by a dealer of numerous and valuable regular customers—is always an important element in merchandising. But in the business of selling bonds and stocks, it is of exceptional value, for the very reason that the small investor relies so largely upon the banker's judgment. This confidential relation of the banker to customers—and the knowledge of the customers' private affairs acquired incidentally—

is often a determining factor in the marketing of securities. With the advent of Big Business such good-will possessed by the older banking houses, preëminently J. P. Morgan & Co. and their Philadelphia House called Drexel & Co., by Lee, Higginson & Co. and Kidder, Peabody, & Co. of Boston, and by Kuhn, Loeb & Co. of New York, became of enhanced importance. The volume of new security issues was greatly increased by huge railroad consolidations, the development of the holding companies, and particularly by the formation of industrial trusts. The rapidly accumulating savings of our people sought investment. The field of operations for the dealer in securities was thus much enlarged. And, as the securities were new and untried, the services of the investment banker were in great demand, and his powers and profits increased accordingly.

CONTROLLING THE SECURITY MAKERS

But this enlargement of their legitimate field of operations did not satisfy investment bankers. They were not content merely to deal in securities. They desired to manufacture them also. They became promoters, or allied themselves with promoters. Thus it was that J. P. Morgan &

Company formed the Steel Trust, the Harvester Trust and the Shipping Trust. And, adding the duties of undertaker to those of midwife, the investment bankers became, in times of corporate disaster, members of security-holders' "Protective Committees"; then they participated as "Reorganization Managers" in the reincarnation of the unsuccessful corporations and ultimately became directors. It was in this way that the Morgan associates acquired their hold upon the Southern Railway, the Northern Pacific, the Reading, the Erie, the Père Marquette, the Chicago and Great Western, and the Cincinnati, Hamilton & Dayton. Often they insured the continuance of such control by the device of the voting trust; but even where no voting trust was created, a secure hold was acquired upon reorganization. It was in this way also that Kuhn, Loeb & Co. became potent in the Union Pacific and in the Baltimore & Ohio.

But the banker's participation in the management of corporations was not limited to cases of promotion or reorganization. An urgent or extensive need of new money was considered a sufficient reason for the banker's entering a board of directors. Often without even such excuse the investment banker has secured a place upon the Board of Directors, through his powerful influence or the control of his customers' proxies. Such seems to have been the fatal entrance of Mr. Morgan into the management of the then prosperous New York, New Haven & Hartford Railroad, in 1892. When once a banker has entered the Board—whatever may have been the occasion—his grip proves tenacious and his influence usually supreme; for he controls the supply of new money.

The investment banker is naturally on the lookout for good bargains in bonds and stocks. Like other merchants, he wants to buy his merchandise cheap. But when he becomes director of a corporation, he occupies a position which prevents the transaction by which he acquires its corporate securities from being properly called a bargain. Can there be real bargaining where the same man is on both sides of a trade? The investment banker, through his controlling influence on the Board of Directors, decides that the corporation shall issue and sell the securities, decides the price at which it shall sell them, and decides that it shall sell the securities to himself. The fact that there are other directors besides the banker on the Board does not, in practice, prevent this being the result. The banker, who holds the purse-strings, becomes usually the dominant spirit. Through voting-trusteeships, exclusive financial agencies, membership on executive or finance committees, or by mere directorships, J. P. Morgan & Co., and their associates, held such financial power in at least thirty-two transportation systems, public utility corporations and industrial companies—companies with an aggregate capitalization of $17,-273,000,000. Mainly for corporations so controlled, J. P. Morgan & Co. procured the public marketing in ten years of security issues aggregating $1,950,000,000. This huge sum does not include any issues marketed privately, nor any issues, however marketed, of intra-state corporations. Kuhn, Loeb & Co. and a few other investment bankers exercise similar control over many other corporations.

CONTROLLING SECURITY BUYERS

Such control of railroads, public service and industrial corporations assures to the investment bankers an ample supply of securities at attractive prices; and merchandise well bought is half sold. But these bond and stock merchants are not disposed to take even a slight risk as to their ability to market their goods.   They saw that if they could control the security-buyers, as well as the security-makers, investment banking would, indeed, be "a happy hunting ground"; and they have made it so.

The numerous small investors cannot, in the strict sense, be controlled; but their dependence upon the banker insures their being duly influenced. A large part, however, of all bonds issued and of many stocks are bought by the prominent corporate investors; and most prominent among these are the life insurance companies, the trust companies, and the banks. The purchase of a security by these institutions not only relieves the banker of the merchandise, but recommends it strongly to the small investor, who believes that these institutions are wisely managed. These controlled corporate investors are not only large customers, but may be particularly accommodating ones. Individual investors are moody. They buy only when they want to do so.   They are sometimes inconveniently reluctant.   Corporate investors, if controlled, may be made to buy when the bankers need a market.   It was natural that the investment bankers proceeded to get control of the great life insurance companies, as well as of the trust companies and the banks.

The field thus occupied is uncommonly rich. The life insurance companies are our leading institutions for savings. Their huge surplus and reserves, augmented daily, are always clamoring for investment. No panic or money shortage stops the inflow of new money from the perennial stream of premiums on existing policies and interest on existing investments. The three great companies—the New York Life, the Mutual of New York, and the Equitable—would have over $55,000,000 of *new* money to invest annually, even if they did not issue a single new policy. In 1904—just before the Armstrong investigation—these three companies had together $1,247,-331,738.18 of assets. They had issued in that year $1,025,671,126 of new policies. The New York legislature placed in 1906 certain restrictions upon their growth; so that their new business since has averaged $547,384,212, or only fifty-three per cent. of what it was in 1904. But the aggregate assets of these companies increased in the last eight years to $1,817,052,260.36. At the time of the Armstrong investigation the average age of these three companies was fifty-six years. *The growth of assets in the last eight years was about half as large as the total growth in the preceding fifty-six years.* These three companies must invest annually about $70,000,000 of new money; and besides, many old investments expire or are changed and the proceeds must be reinvested. A large part of all life insurance surplus and reserves are invested in bonds. The aggregate bond investments of these three companies on January 1, 1913, was $1,019,153,268.93.

It was natural that the investment bankers should seek to control these never-failing reservoirs of capital. George W. Perkins was Vice-President of the New York Life, the largest of the companies. While remaining such he was made a partner in J. P. Morgan & Co., and in the four years preceding the Armstrong investigation, his firm sold the New York Life $38,804,918.51 in securities. The New York Life is a mutual company, supposed to be controlled by its policy-holders. But, as the Pujo Committee funds "the so-called control of life insurance companies by policy-holders through mutualization is a farce" and "its only result is to keep in office a self-constituted, self-perpetuating management."

The Equitable Life Assurance Society is a stock company and is controlled by $100,000 of stock. The dividend on this stock is limited by law to seven per cent.; but in 1910 Mr. Morgan paid about $3,000,000 for $51,000, par value of this stock, or $5,882.35 a share. The dividend return on the stock investment is less than one-eighth of one per cent.; but the assets controlled amount now to over $500,000,000. And certain of these assets had an especial value for investment bankers;—namely, the large holdings of stock in banks and trust companies.

The Armstrong investigation disclosed the extent of financial power exerted through the insurance company holdings of bank and trust company stock. The Committee recommended legislation compelling the insurance companies to dispose of the stock within five years. A law to that effect was enacted, but the time was later extended. The companies then disposed of a part of their bank and trust company stocks; but, as the insurance companies were controlled by the investment bankers, these gentlemen sold the bank and trust company stocks to themselves.

Referring to such purchases from the Mutual Life, as well as from the Equitable, the Pujo Committee found:

"Here, then, were stocks of five important trust companies and one of our largest national banks in New York City that had been held by these two life insurance companies. Within five years all of these stocks, so far as distributed by the insurance companies, have found their way into the hands of the men who virtually controlled or were identified with the management of the insurance companies or of their close allies and associates, to that extent thus further entrenching them."

The banks and trust companies are depositaries, in the main, not of the people's savings, but of the business man's quick capital. Yet, since the investment banker acquired control of banks and trust companies, these institutions also have become, like the life companies, large purchasers of bonds and stocks. Many of our national banks have invested in this manner a large part of all their resources, including capital, surplus and deposits. The bond investments of some banks exceed by far the aggregate of their capital and surplus, and nearly equal their loanable deposits.

CONTROLLING OTHER PEOPLE'S QUICK CAPITAL

The goose that lays golden eggs has been considered a most valuable possession. But even more profitable is the privilege of taking the

golden eggs laid by somebody else's goose.
The investment bankers and their associates now
enjoy that privilege. They control the people
through the people's own money. If the bankers' power were commensurate only with their
wealth, they would have relatively little influence
on American business. Vast fortunes like those
of the Astors are no doubt regrettable. They
are inconsistent with democracy. They are un-
social. And they seem peculiarly unjust when
they represent largely unearned increment. But
the wealth of the Astors does not endanger
political or industrial liberty. It is insignificant
in amount as compared with the aggregate wealth
of America, or even of New York City. It lacks
significance largely because its owners have only
the income from their own wealth. The Astor
wealth is static. The wealth of the Morgan
associates is dynamic. The power and the
growth of power of our financial oligarchs comes
from wielding the savings and quick capital of
others. In two of the three great life insurance
companies the influence of J. P. Morgan & Co.
and their associates is exerted without any individual investment by them whatsoever. Even
in the Equitable, where Mr. Morgan bought an
actual majority of all the outstanding stock, his

investment amounts to little more than one-half of one per cent. of the assets of the company. The fetters which bind the people are forged from the people's own gold.

But the reservoir of other people's money, from which the investment bankers now draw their greatest power, is not the life insurance companies, but the banks and the trust companies. Bank deposits represent the really quick capital of the nation. They are the life blood of businesses. Their effective force is much greater than that of an equal amount of wealth permanently invested. The 34 banks and trust companies, which the Pujo Committee declared to be directly controlled by the Morgan associates, held $1,983,-000,000 in deposits. Control of these institutions means the ability to lend a large part of these funds, directly and indirectly, to themselves; and what is often even more important, the power to prevent the funds being lent to any rival interests. These huge deposits can, in the discretion of those in control, be used to meet the temporary needs of their subject corporations. When bonds and stocks are issued to finance permanently these corporations, the bank deposits can, in large part, be loaned by the investment bankers in control to themselves and their associates; so that securities bought may be carried by them, until sold to investors. Or these bank deposits may be loaned to allied bankers, or jobbers in securities, or to speculators, to enable them to carry the bonds or stocks. Easy money tends to make securities rise in the market. Tight money nearly always makes them fall. The control by the leading investment bankers over the banks and trust companies is so great, that they can often determine, for a time, the market for money by lending or refusing to lend on the Stock Exchange. In this way, among others, they have power to affect the general trend of prices in bonds and stocks. Their power over a particular security is even greater. Its sale on the market may depend upon whether the security is favored or discriminated against when offered to the banks and trust companies, as collateral for loans.

Furthermore, it is the investment banker's access to other people's money in controlled banks and trust companies which alone enables any individual banking concern to take so large part of the annual output of bonds and stocks. The banker's own capital, however large, would soon be exhausted. And even the loanable funds of the banks would often be exhausted, but for the large deposits made in those banks by the life insurance, railroad, public service, and industrial corporations which the bankers also control. On December 31, 1912, the three leading life insurance companies had deposits in banks and trust companies aggregating $13,839,-189.08. As the Pujo Committee finds:

"The men who through their control over the funds of our railroads and industrial companies are able to direct where such funds shall be kept and thus to create these great reservoirs of the people's money, are the ones who are in position to tap those reservoirs for the ventures in which they are interested and to prevent their being tapped for purposes of which they do not approve. The latter is quite as important a factor as the former. It is the controlling consideration in its effect on competition in the railroad and industrial world."

HAVING YOUR CAKE AND EATING IT TOO

But the power of the investment banker over other people's money is often more direct and effective than that exerted through controlled banks and trust companies. J. P. Morgan & Co. achieve the supposedly impossible feat of having

their cake and eating it too.   They buy the bonds
and stocks of controlled railroads and industrial
concerns, and pay the purchase price; and still
do not part with their money.   This is accomplished by the simple device of becoming the bank
of deposit of the controlled corporations, instead
of having the company deposit in some merely
controlled bank in whose operation others have
at least some share.   When J. P. Morgan & Co.
buy an issue of securities the purchase money,
instead of being paid over to the corporation, is
retained by the banker for the corporation, to
be drawn upon only as the funds are needed by
the corporation.   And as the securities are issued
in large blocks, and the money raised is often not
all spent until long thereafter, the aggregate of
the balances remaining in the banker's hands are
huge.   Thus J. P. Morgan & Co. (including their
Philadelphia house, called Drexel & Co.) held
on November 1, 1912, deposits aggregating
$162,491,819.65.

POWER AND PELF

The operations of so comprehensive a system
of concentration necessarily developed in the
bankers overweening power.   And the bankers'
power grows by what it feeds on.   Power begets

wealth; and added wealth opens ever new opportunities for the acquisition of wealth and power. The operations of these bankers are so vast and numerous that even a very reasonable compensation for the service performed by the bankers, would, in the aggregate, produce for them incomes so large as to result in huge accumulations of capital. But the compensation taken by the bankers as commissions or profits is often far from reasonable. Occupying, as they so frequently do, the inconsistent position of being at the same time seller and buyer, the standard for so-called compensation actually applied, is not the "Rule of reason", but "All the traffic will bear." And this is true even where there is no sinister motive. The weakness of human nature prevents men from being good judges of their own deservings.

The syndicate formed by J. P. Morgan & Co. to underwrite the United States Steel Corporation took for its services securities which netted $62,500,000 in cash. Of this huge sum J. P. Morgan & Co. received, as syndicate managers, $12,500,000 in addition to the share which they were entitled to receive as syndicate members. This sum of $62,500,000 was only a part of the fees paid for the service of monopolizing the steel industry. In addition to the commissions taken specifically for organizing the United States Steel Corporation, large sums were paid for organizing the several companies of which it is composed. For instance, the National Tube Company was capitalized at $80,000,000 of stock; $40,000,000 of which was common stock. Half of this $40,000,000 was taken by J. P. Morgan & Co. and their associates for promotion services; and the $20,000,000 stock so taken became later exchangeable for $25,000,000 of Steel Common. Commissioner of Corporations Herbert Knox Smith, found that:

"More than $150,000,000 of the stock of the Steel Corporation was issued directly or indirectly (through exchange) for mere promotion or underwriting services. In other words, nearly one-seventh of the total capital stock of the Steel Corporation appears to have been issued directly or indirectly to promoters' services."

The so-called fees and commissions taken by the bankers and associates upon the organization of the trusts have been exceptionally large. But even after the trusts are successfully launched the exactions of the bankers are often extortionate. The syndicate which underwrote, in 1901, the Steel Corporation's preferred stock conversion plan, advanced only $20,000,000 in cash and received an underwriting commission of $6,800,000.

The exaction of huge commissions is not confined to trust and other industrial concerns. The Interborough Railway is a most prosperous corporation. It earned last year nearly 21 per cent. on its capital stock, and secured from New York City, in connection with the subway extension, a very favorable contract. But when it financed its $170,000,000 bond issue it was agreed that J. P. Morgan & Co. should receive three per cent., that is, $5,100,000, for merely forming this syndicate. More recently, the New York, New Haven & Hartford Railroad agreed to pay J. P. Morgan & Co. a commission of $1,680,000; that is, 2 1/2 per cent., to form a syndicate to underwrite an issue at par of $67,000,000 20-year 6 per cent. convertible debentures. That means: The bankers bound themselves to take at 97 1/2 any of these six per cent. convertible bonds which stockholders might be unwilling to buy at 100. When the contract was made the New Haven's then outstanding six per cent. convertible bonds were selling at 114. And the

new issue, as soon as announced, was in such
demand that the public offered and was for
months willing to buy at 106 bonds which the
Company were to pay J. P. Morgan & Co. $1,-
680,000 to be willing to take at par.

WHY THE BANKS BECAME INVESTMENT BANKERS

These large profits from promotions, underwritings and security purchases led to a revolutionary change in the conduct of our leading
banking institutions. It was obvious that control by the investment bankers of the deposits
in banks and trust companies was an essential
element in their securing these huge profits.
And the bank officers naturally asked, "Why
then should not the banks and trust companies
share in so profitable a field? Why should not
they themselves become investment bankers
too, with all the new functions incident to 'Big
Business'?" To do so would involve a de-
parture from the legitimate sphere of the
banking business, which is the making of temporary loans to business concerns. But the
temptation was irresistible. The invasion of
the investment banker into the banks' field of
operation was followed by a counter invasion
by the banks into the realm of the investment

banker. Most prominent among the banks were the National City and the First National of New York. But theirs was not a hostile invasion. The contending forces met as allies, joined forces to control the business of the country, and to "divide the spoils." The alliance was cemented by voting trusts, by interlocking directorates and by joint ownerships. There resulted the fullest "cooperation"; and ever more railroads, public service corporations, and industrial concerns were brought into complete subjection.

CHAPTER II

HOW THE COMBINERS COMBINE

AMONG the allies, two New York banks—
the National City and the First National—
stand preëminent. They constitute, with the
Morgan firm, the inner group of the Money
Trust. Each of the two banks, like J. P. Morgan & Co., has huge resources. Each of the
two banks, like the firm of J. P. Morgan & Co.,
has been dominated by a genius in combination.
In the National City it is James Stillman; in
the First National, George F. Baker. Each of
these gentlemen was formerly President, and is
now Chairman of the Board of Directors. The
resources of the National City Bank (including
its Siamese-twin security company) are about
$300,000,000; those of the First National Bank
(including its Siamese-twin security company)
are about $200,000,000. The resources of the
Morgan firm have not been disclosed. But it
appears that they have available for their operations, also, huge deposits from their subjects;
deposits reported as $162,500,000.

The private fortunes of the chief actors in the combination have not been ascertained. But sporadic evidence indicates how great are the possibilities of accumulation when one has the use of "other people's money." Mr. Morgan's wealth became proverbial. Of Mr. Stillman's many investments, only one was specifically referred to, as he was in Europe during the investigation, and did not testify. But that one is significant. His 47,498 shares in the National City Bank are worth about $18,000,000. Mr. Jacob H. Schiff aptly described this as "a very nice investment."

Of Mr. Baker's investments we know more, as he testified on many subjects. His 20,000 shares in the First National Bank are worth at least $20,000,000. His stocks in six other New York banks and trust companies are together worth about $3,000,000. The scale of his investment in railroads may be inferred from his former holdings in the Central Railroad of New Jersey. He was its largest stockholder—so large that with a few friends he held a majority of the $27,436,800 par value of outstanding stock, which the Reading bought at $160 a share. He is a director in 28 other railroad companies; and presumably a stockholder in, at least, as

many. The full extent of his fortune was not
inquired into, for that was not an issue in the
investigation. But it is not surprising that Mr.
Baker saw little need of new laws. When asked:
   "You think everything is all right as it is
in this world, do you not?"
   He answered:
   "Pretty nearly."

RAMIFICATIONS OF POWER

   But wealth expressed in figures gives a wholly
inadequate picture of the allies' power. Their
wealth is dynamic. It is wielded by geniuses
in combination. It finds its proper expression
in means of control. To comprehend the power
of the allies we must try to visualize the ramifi-
cations through which the forces operate.
   Mr. Baker is a director in 22 corporations
having, with their many subsidiaries, aggregate
resources or capitalization of $7,272,000,000.
But the direct and visible power of the First
National Bank, which Mr. Baker dominates,
extends further. The Pujo report shows that
its directors (including Mr. Baker's son) are
directors in at least 27 other corporations
with resources of $4,270,000,000. That is, the
First National is represented in 49 corporations,

with aggregate resources or capitalization of $11,542,000,000.

It may help to an appreciation of the allies' power to name a few of the more prominent corporations in which, for instance, Mr. Baker's influence is exerted—visibly and directly—as voting trustee, executive committee man or simple director.

1. *Banks, Trust, and Life Insurance Companies:* First National Bank of New York; National Bank of Commerce; Farmers' Loan and Trust Company; Mutual Life Insurance Company.

2. *Railroad Companies:* New York Central Lines; New Haven, Reading, Erie, Lackawanna, Lehigh Valley, Southern, Northern Pacific, Chicago, Burlington & Quincy.

3. *Public Service Corporations:* American Telegraph & Telephone Company, Adams Express Company.

4. *Industrial Corporations:* United States Steel Corporation, Pullman Company.

Mr. Stillman is a director in only 7 corporations, with aggregate assets of $2,476,000,000; but the directors in the National City Bank, which he dominates, are directors in at least 41 other corporations which, with their subsidiaries, have an aggregate capitalization or resources of $10,564,000,000. The members of the firm of J. P. Morgan & Co., the acknowledged leader of the allied forces, hold 72 directorships in 47 of the largest corporations of the country.

The Pujo Committee finds that the members of J. P. Morgan & Co. and the directors of their controlled trust companies and of the First National and the National City Bank together hold:

"One hundred and eighteen directorships in 34 banks and trust companies having total resources of $2,679,000,000 and total deposits of $1,983,000,000.

"Thirty directorships in 10 insurance companies having total assets of $2,293,000,000.

"One hundred and five directorships in 32 transportation systems having a total capitalization of $11,784,000,000 and a total mileage (excluding express companies and steamship lines) of 150,200.

"Sixty-three directorships in 24 producing and trading corporations having a total capitalization of $3,339,000,000.

"Twenty-five directorships in 12 public-utility corporations having a total capitalization of $2,150,000,000.

"In all, 341 directorships in 112 corporations having aggregate resources or capitalization of $22,245,000,000."

TWENTY-TWO BILLION DOLLARS

"Twenty-two billion dollars is a large sum— so large that we have difficulty in grasping its significance. The mind realizes size only through comparisons. With what can we compare twenty-two billions of dollars? Twenty-two billions of dollars is more than three times the assessed value of all the property, real and personal, in all New England. It is nearly three times the assessed value of all the real estate in the City of New York. It is more than twice the assessed value of all the property in the thirteen Southern states. It is more than the assessed value of all the property in the twenty-two states, north and south, lying west of the Mississippi River.

But the huge sum of twenty-two billion dollars is not large enough to include all the corporations to which the "influence" of the three allies, directly and visibly, extends, for

First: There are 56 other corporations (not included in the Pujo schedule) each with capital or resources of over $5,000,000, and aggregating nearly $1,350,000,000, in which the Morgan allies are represented according to the directories of directors.

Second: The Pujo schedule does not include any corporation with resources of less than $5,000,000. But these financial giants have shown their humility by becoming directors in many such. For instance, members of J. P. Morgan & Co., and directors in the National City Bank and the First National Bank are also directors in 158 such corporations. Available publications disclose the capitalization of only 38 of these, but those 38 aggregate $78,669,375.

Third: The Pujo schedule includes only the corporations in which the Morgan associates actually appear by name as directors. It does not include those in which they are represented by dummies, or otherwise. For instance, the Morgan influence certainly extends to the Kansas City Terminal Railway Company, for which they have marketed since 1910 (in connection with others) four issues aggregating $41,761,000. But no member of J. P. Morgan & Co., of the National City Bank, or of the First National Bank appears on the Kansas City Terminal directorate.

Fourth: The Pujo schedule does not include

all the subsidiaries of the corporations scheduled. For instance, the capitalization of the New Haven System is given as $385,000,000. That sum represents the bond and stock capital of the New Haven *Railroad*. But the New Haven *System* comprises many controlled corporations whose capitalization is only to a slight extent included directly or indirectly in the New Haven Railroad balance sheet. The New Haven, like most large corporations, is a holding company also; and a holding company may control subsidiaries while owning but a small part of the latters' outstanding securities. Only the small part so held will be represented in the holding company's balance sheet. Thus, while the New Haven Railroad's capitalization is only $385,000,000—and that sum only appears in the Pujo schedule—the capitalization of the New Haven System, as shown by a chart submitted to the Committee, is over twice as great; namely, $849,000,000.

It is clear, therefore, that the $22,000,000,000, referred to by the Pujo Committee, understates the extent of concentration effected by the inner group of the Money Trust.

CEMENTING THE TRIPLE ALLIANCE

Care was taken by these builders of imperial power that their structure should be enduring. It has been buttressed on every side by joint ownerships and mutual stockholdings, as well as by close personal relationships; for directorships are ephemeral and may end with a new election. Mr. Morgan and his partners acquired one-sixth of the stock of the First National Bank, and made a $6,000,000 investment in the stock of the National City Bank. Then J. P. Morgan & Co., the National City, and the First National (or their dominant officers—Mr. Stillman and Mr. Baker) acquired together, by stock purchases and voting trusts, control of the National Bank of Commerce, with its $190,000,000 of resources; of the Chase National, with $125,000,000; of the Guaranty Trust Company, with $232,000,000; of the Bankers' Trust Company, with $205,000,-000; and of a number of smaller, but important, financial institutions. They became joint voting trustees in great railroad systems; and finally (as if the allies were united into a single concern) loyal and efficient service in the banks—like that rendered by Mr. Davison and Mr. Lamont in the First National—was rewarded by promotion

to membership in the firm of J. P. Morgan
& Co.

THE PROVINCIAL ALLIES

Thus equipped and bound together, J. P.
Morgan & Co., the National City and the First
National easily dominated America's financial
center, New York; for certain other important
bankers, to be hereafter mentioned, were held
in restraint by "gentlemen's" agreements.
The three allies dominated Philadelphia too;
for the firm of Drexel & Co. is J. P. Morgan &
Co. under another name. But there are two
other important money centers in America,
Boston and Chicago.

In Boston there are two large international
banking houses—Lee, Higginson & Co., and
Kidder, Peabody & Co.—both long established
and rich; and each possessing an extensive,
wealthy clientele of eager investors in bonds and
stocks. Since 1907 each of these firms has purchased or underwritten (principally in conjunction with other bankers) about 100 different
security issues of the greater interstate corporations, the issues of each banker amounting in
the aggregate to over $1,000,000,000. Concen-
tration of banking capital has proceeded even

further in Boston than in New York. By successive consolidations the number of national banks has been reduced from 58 in 1898 to 19 in 1913. There are in Boston now also 23 trust companies.

The National Shawmut Bank, the First National Bank of Boston and the Old Colony Trust Co., which these two Boston banking houses and their associates control, alone have aggregate resources of $288,386,294, constituting about one-half of the banking resources of the city. These great banking institutions, which are themselves the result of many consolidations, and the 21 other banks and trust companies, in which their directors are also directors, hold together 90 per cent. of the total banking resources of Boston. And linked to them by interlocking directorates are 9 other banks and trust companies whose aggregate resources are about 2 1/2 per cent. of Boston's total. Thus of 42 banking institutions, 33, with aggregate resources of $560,516,239, holding about 92 1/2 per cent. of the aggregate banking resources of Boston, are interlocked. But even the remaining 9 banks and trust companies, which together hold but 7 1/2 per cent. of Boston banking resources, are not all independent of one another. Three are linked together; so that there appear to be only six banks in all Boston that are free from interlocking directorate relations. They together represent but 5 per cent. of Boston's banking resources. And it may well be doubted whether all of even those 6 are entirely free from affiliation with the other groups.

Boston's banking concentration is not limited to the legal confines of the city. Around Boston proper are over thirty suburbs, which with it form what is popularly known as "Greater Boston." These suburban municipalities, and also other important cities like Worcester and Springfield, are, in many respects, within Boston's "sphere of influence." Boston's inner banking group has interlocked, not only 33 of the 42 banks of Boston proper, as above shown, but has linked with them, by interlocking directorships, at least 42 other banks and trust companies in 35 other municipalities.

Once Lee, Higginson & Co. and Kidder, Peabody & Co. were active competitors. They are so still in some small, or purely local matters; but both are devoted co-operators with the Morgan associates in larger and interstate transactions; and the alliance with these great Boston banking houses has been cemented by mutual

stockholdings and co-directorships. Financial
concentration seems to have found its highest expression in Boston.

Somewhat similar relations exist between the
triple alliance and Chicago's great financial institutions—its First National Bank, the Illinois
Trust and Savings Bank, and the Continental
& Commercial National Bank—which together
control resources of $561,000,000. And similar
relations would doubtless be found to exist with
the leading bankers of the other important financial centers of America, as to which the Pujo
Committee was prevented by lack of time from
making investigation.

THE AUXILIARIES

Such are the primary, such the secondary
powers which comprise the Money Trust; but
these are supplemented by forces of magnitude.

"Radiating from these principal groups," says
the Pujo Committee, "and closely affiliated with
them are smaller but important banking houses,
such as Kissel, Kinnicut & Co., White, Weld
& Co., and Harvey Fisk & Sons, who receive
large and lucrative patronage from the dominat-
ing groups, and are used by the latter as jobbers
or distributors of securities, the issuing of which

they control, but which for reasons of their own they prefer not to have issued or distributed under their own names. Lee, Higginson & Co., besides being partners with the inner group, are also frequently utilized in this service because of their facilities as distributors of securities."

For instance, J. P. Morgan & Co. as fiscal agents of the New Haven Railroad had the right to market its securities and that of its subsidiaries. Among the numerous New Haven subsidiaries, is the New York, Westchester and Boston—the road which cost $1,500,000 a mile to build, and which earned a *deficit* last year of nearly $1,500,000, besides failing to earn any return upon the New Haven's own stock and bond investment of $8,241,951. When the New Haven concluded to market $17,200,000 of these bonds, J. P. Morgan & Co., "for reasons of their own," "preferred not to have these bonds issued or distributed under their own name." The Morgan firm took the bonds at 92 1/2 net; and the bonds were marketed by Kissel, Kinnicut & Co. and others at 96 1/4.

THE SATELLITES

The alliance is still further supplemented, as the Pujo Committee shows:

"Beyond these inner groups and sub-groups are banks and bankers throughout the country who co-operate with them in underwriting or guaranteeing the sale of securities offered to the public, and who also act as distributors of such securities. It was impossible to learn the identity of these corporations, owing to the unwillingness of the members of the inner group to disclose the names of their underwriters, but sufficient appears to justify the statement that there are at least hundreds of them and that they extend into many of the cities throughout this and foreign countries.

"The patronage thus proceeding from the inner group and its sub-groups is of great value to these banks and bankers, who are thus tied by self-interest to the great issuing houses and may be regarded as a part of this vast financial organization. Such patronage yields no inconsiderable part of the income of these banks and bankers and without much risk on account of the facilities of the principal groups for placing issues of securities through their domination of great banks and trust companies and their other domestic affiliations and their foreign connections. The underwriting commissions on issues made by this inner group are usually easily earned and do not ordinarily involve the underwriters in the purchase of the underwritten securities. Their interest in the transaction is generally adjusted unless they choose to purchase part of the securities, by the payment to them of a commission. There are, however, occasions on which this is not the case. The underwriters are then required to take the securities. Bankers and brokers are so anxious to be permitted to participate in these transactions under the lead of the inner group that as a rule they join when invited to do so, regardless of their approval of the particular business, lest by refusing they should thereafter cease to be invited."

In other words, an invitation from these royal bankers is interpreted as a command. As a result, these great bankers frequently get huge commissions without themselves distributing any of the bonds, or ever having taken any actual risk.

"In the case of the New York subway financing of $170,000,000 of bonds by Messrs. Morgan & Co. and their associates, Mr. Davison [as the Pujo Committee reports] estimated that there were from 100 to 125 such underwriters who were apparently glad to agree that Messrs.

Morgan & Co., the First National Bank, and the
National City Bank should receive 3 per cent.,
—equal to $5,100,000—for forming this syndi-
cate, thus relieving themselves from all liability,
whilst the underwriters assumed the risk of what
the bonds would realize and of being required to
take their share of the unsold portion.''

THE PROTECTION OF PSEUDO-ETHICS

The organization of the Money Trust is intensive, the combination comprehensive; but
one other element was recognized as necessary
to render it stable, and to make its dynamic force
irresistible.   Despotism, be it financial or political, is vulnerable, unless it is believed to rest
upon a moral sanction.   The longing for freedom
is ineradicable.   It will express itself in protest
against servitude and inaction, unless the striving for freedom be made to seem immoral.
Long ago monarchs invented, as a preservative
of absolutism, the fiction of ''The divine right of
kings.''   Bankers, imitating royalty, invented recently that precious rule of so-called ''Ethics,'' by
which it is declared unprofessional to come to the
financial relief of any corporation which is already
the prey of another ''reputable'' banker.

''The possibility of competition between these

banking houses in the purchase of securities,"
says the Pujo Committee, "is further removed
by the understanding between them and others,
that one will not seek, by offering better terms,
to take away from another, a customer which it
has theretofore served, and by corollary of this,
namely, that where given bankers have once
satisfactorily united in bringing out an issue of
a corporation, they shall also join in bringing
out any subsequent issue of the same corporations. This is described as a principle of banking
ethics."

The "Ethical" basis of the rule must be that
the interests of the combined bankers are
superior to the interests of the rest of the community. Their attitude reminds one of the
"spheres of influence" with ample "hinterlands"
by which rapacious nations are adjusting differ-
ences. Important banking concerns, too ambitious to be willing to take a subordinate position
in the alliance, and too powerful to be suppressed,
are accorded a financial "sphere of influence"
upon the understanding that the rule of banking
ethics will be faithfully observed. Most prominent among such lesser potentates are Kuhn,
Loeb & Co., of New York, an international
banking house of great wealth, with large clientele

and connections. They are accorded an important "sphere of influence" in American rail-roading, including among other systems the Baltimore & Ohio, the Union Pacific and the Southern Pacific. They and the Morgan group have with few exceptions preëmpted the banking business of the important railroads of the country. But even Kuhn, Loeb & Co. are not wholly independent. The Pujo Committee reports that they are "qualified allies of the inner group"; and through their "close relations with the National City Bank and the National Bank of Commerce and other financial institutions" have "many interests in common with the Morgan associates, conducting large joint-account operations with them."

THE EVILS RESULTANT

First: These banker-barons levy, through their excessive exactions, a heavy toll upon the whole community; upon owners of money for leave to invest it; upon railroads, public service and industrial companies, for leave to use this money of other people; and, through these corporations, upon consumers.

"The charge of capital," says the Pujo Committee, "which of course enters universally into

the price of commodities and of service, is thus
in effect determined by agreement amongst those
supplying it and not under the check of competition. If there be any virtue in the principle of
competition, certainly any plan or arrangement
which prevents its operation in the performance
of so fundamental a commercial function as the
supplying of capital is peculiarly injurious."

Second: More serious, however, is the effect
of the Money Trust in directly suppressing competition. That suppression enables the monopo-
list to extort excessive profits; but monopoly
increases the burden of the consumer even more
in other ways. Monopoly arrests development;
and through arresting development, prevents
that lessening of the cost of production and of
distribution which would otherwise take place.

Can full competition exist among the anthracite coal railroads when the Morgan associates
are potent in all of them? And with like
conditions prevailing, what competition is to be
expected between the Northern Pacific and the
Great Northern, the Southern, the Louisville
and Nashville, and the Atlantic Coast Line; or
between the Westinghouse Manufacturing Company and the General Electric Company? As
the Pujo Committee finds:

"Such affiliations tend as a cover and conduit for secret arrangements and understandings in restriction of competition through the agency of the banking house thus situated."

And under existing conditions of combination, relief through other banking houses is precluded.

"It can hardly be expected that the banks, trust companies, and other institutions that are thus seeking participation from this inner group would be likely to engage in business of a character that would be displeasing to the latter or would interfere with their plans or prestige. And so the protection that can be afforded by the members of the inner group constitutes the safest refuge of our great industrial combinations against future competition. The powerful grip of these gentlemen is upon the throttle that controls the wheels of credit, and upon their signal those wheels will turn or stop."

Third: But far more serious even than the suppression of competition is the suppression of industrial liberty, indeed of manhood itself, which this overweening financial power entails. The intimidation which it effects extends far beyond "the banks, trust companies, and other institutions seeking participation from this inner group in their lucrative underwritings"; and far beyond those interested in the great corporations directly dependent upon the inner group. Its blighting and benumbing effect extends as well to the small and seemingly independent business man, to the vast army of professional men and others directly dependent upon "Big Business," and to many another; for

1. Nearly every enterprising business man needs bank credit. The granting of credit involves the exercise of judgment of the bank officials; and however honestly the bank officials may wish to exercise their discretion, experience shows that their judgment is warped by the existence of the all-pervading power of the Money Trust. He who openly opposes the great interests will often be found to lack that quality of "safe and sane"-ness which is the basis of financial credit.

2. Nearly every enterprising business man and a large part of our professional men have something to sell to, or must buy something from, the great corporations to which the control or influence of the money lords extends directly, or from or to affiliated interests. Sometimes it is merchandise; sometimes it is service; sometimes

they have nothing either to buy or to sell, but
desire political or social advancement. Sometimes they want merely peace. Experience shows
that "it is not healthy to buck against a locomotive," and "Business is business."

Here and there you will find a hero,—red-
blooded, and courageous,—loving manhood more
than wealth, place or security,—who dared to
fight for independence and won. Here and there
you may find the martyr, who resisted in silence
and suffered with resignation. But America,
which seeks "the greatest good of the greatest
number," cannot be content with conditions that
fit only the hero, the martyr or the slave.

CHAPTER III

INTERLOCKING DIRECTORATES

The practice of interlocking directorates is the root of many evils. It offends laws human and divine. Applied to rival corporations, it tends to the suppression of competition and to violation of the Sherman law. Applied to corporations which deal with each other, it tends to disloyalty and to violation of the fundamental law that no man can serve two masters. In either event it tends to inefficiency; for it removes incentive and destroys soundness of judgment. It is undemocratic, for it rejects the platform: "A fair field and no favors,"—substituting the pull of privilege for the push of manhood. It is the most potent instrument of the Money Trust. Break the control so exercised by the investment bankers over railroads, public-service and industrial corporations, over banks, life insurance and trust companies, and a long step will have been taken toward attainment of the New Freedom.

The term "Interlocking directorates" is here used in a broad sense as including all intertwined conflicting interests, whatever the form, and by whatever device effected. The objection extends alike to contracts of a corporation whether with one of its directors individually, or with a firm of which he is a member, or with another corporation in which he is interested as an officer or director or stockholder. The objection extends likewise to men holding the inconsistent position of director in two potentially competing corporations, even if those corporations do not actually deal with each other.

THE ENDLESS CHAIN

A single example will illustrate the vicious circle of control—the endless chain—through which our financial oligarchy now operates:

J. P. Morgan (or a partner), a director of the New York, New Haven & Hartford Railroad, causes that company to sell to J. P. Morgan & Co. an issue of bonds. J. P. Morgan & Co. borrow the money with which to pay for the bonds from the Guaranty Trust Company, of which Mr. Morgan (or a partner) is a director. J. P. Morgan & Co. sell the bonds to the Penn Mutual Life Insurance Company, of which Mr. Morgan (or a partner) is a director. The New Haven spends the proceeds of the bonds in purchasing steel rails from the United States Steel Corporation, of which Mr. Morgan (or a partner) is a director. The United States Steel Corporation spends the proceeds of the rails in purchasing electrical supplies from the General Electric Company, of which Mr. Morgan (or a partner) is a director. The General Electric sells supplies to the Western Union Telegraph Company, a subsidiary of the American Telephone and Telegraph Company; and in both Mr. Morgan (or a partner) is a director. The Telegraph Company has an exclusive wire contract with the Reading, of which Mr. Morgan (or a partner) is a director. The Reading buys its passenger cars from the Pullman Company, of which Mr. Morgan (or a partner) is a director. The Pullman Company buys (for local use) locomotives from the Baldwin Locomotive Company, of which Mr. Morgan (or a partner) is a director. The Reading, the General Electric, the Steel Corporation and the New Haven, like the Pullman, buy locomotives from the Baldwin Company. The Steel Corporation, the Telephone Company, the New Haven, the Reading, the Pullman and the Baldwin Companies, like the Western Union, buy electrical supplies from the General Electric. The Baldwin, the Pullman, the Reading, the Telephone, the Telegraph and the General Electric companies, like the New Haven, buy steel products from the Steel Corporation. Each and every one of the companies last named markets its securities through J. P. Morgan & Co.; each deposits its funds with J. P. Morgan & Co.; and with these funds of each, the firm enters upon further operations.

This specific illustration is in part supposititious; but it represents truthfully the operation of interlocking directorates. Only it must be multiplied many times and with many permutations to represent fully the extent to which the interests of a few men are intertwined. Instead of taking the New Haven as the railroad starting point in our example, the New York Central, the Santa Fé, the Southern, the Lehigh Valley, the Chicago and Great Western, the Erie or the Père Marquette might have been selected; instead of the Guaranty Trust Company as the banking reservoir, any one of a dozen other important banks or trust companies; instead of the Penn Mutual as purchaser of the bonds, other insurance companies; instead of the General Electric, its qualified competitor, the Westinghouse Electric and Manufacturing Company. The chain is indeed endless; for each controlled corporation is entwined with many others.

As the *nexus* of "Big Business" the Steel Corporation stands, of course, preëminent. The Stanley Committee showed that the few men who control the Steel Corporation, itself an owner of important railroads, are directors also in twenty-nine other railroad systems, with 126,000 miles of line (more than half the railroad mileage of the United States), and in important steamship companies. Through all these alliances and the huge traffic it controls, the Steel Corporation's influence pervades railroad and steamship companies—not as carriers only—but as the largest customers for steel. And its influence with users of steel extends much further. These same few men are also directors in twelve steel-using street railway systems, including some of the largest in the world. They are directors in forty machinery and similar steel-using manufacturing companies; in many gas, oil and water companies, extensive users of iron products; and in the great wire-using telephone and telegraph companies. The aggregate assets of these different corporations—through which these few men exert their influence over the business of the United States—exceeds sixteen billion dollars.

Obviously, interlocking directorates, and all that term implies, must be effectually prohibited before the freedom of American business can be regained. The prohibition will not be an innovation. It will merely give full legal sanction to the fundamental law of morals and of human nature: that "No man can serve two masters." The surprising fact is that a principle of equity so firmly rooted should have been departed from at all in dealing with corporations. For no rule of law has, in other connections, been more rigorously applied, than that which prohibits a trustee from occupying inconsistent positions, from dealing with himself, or from using his fiduciary position for personal profit. And a director of a corporation is as obviously a trustee as persons holding similar positions in an unincorporated association, or in a private trust estate, who are called specifically by that name. The Courts have recognized this fully.

Thus, the Court of Appeals of New York declared in an important case:

"While not technically trustees, for the title of the corporate property was in the corporation itself, they were charged with the duties and subject to the liabilities of trustees. Clothed with the power of controlling the property and managing the affairs of the corporation without let or hindrance, as to third persons, they were its agents; but as to the corporation itself equity holds them liable as trustees. While courts of law generally treat the directors as agents, courts of equity treat them as trustees, and hold them to a strict account for any breach of the trust relation. For all practical purposes they are trustees, when called upon in equity to account for their official conduct."

NULLIFYING THE LAW

But this wholesome rule of business, so clearly laid down, was practically nullified by courts in creating two unfortunate limitations, as concessions doubtless to the supposed needs of commerce.

First: Courts held valid contracts between a corporation and a director, or between two corporations with a common director, where it was shown that in making the contract, the corporation was represented by independent directors and that the vote of the interested director was unnecessary to carry the motion and his presence was not needed to constitute a quorum.

Second: Courts held that even where a com-

mon director participated actively in the making
of a contract between two corporations, the
contract was not absolutely void, but voidable
only at the election of the corporation.

The first limitation ignored the rule of law that
a beneficiary is entitled to disinterested advice
from *all* his trustees, and not merely from some;
and that a trustee may violate his trust by inaction as well as by action. It ignored, also, the
laws of human nature, in assuming that the influence of a director is confined to the act of
voting. Every one knows that the most effective
work is done before any vote is taken, subtly,
and without provable participation. Every one
should know that the denial of minority repre-
sentation on boards of directors has resulted in
the domination of most corporations by one or
two men; and in practically banishing all criticism of the dominant power. And even where
the board is not so dominated, there is too often
that "harmonious cooperation" among directors
which secures for each, in his own line, a due share
of the corporation's favors.

The second limitation—by which contracts,
in the making of which the interested director
participates actively, are held *merely voidable*
instead of absolutely void—ignores the teachings

of experience. To hold such contracts merely voidable has resulted practically in declaring them valid. It is the directors who control corporate action; and there is little reason to expect that any contract, entered into by a board with a fellow director, however unfair, would be subsequently avoided. Appeals from Philip drunk to Philip sober are not of frequent occurrence, nor very fruitful. But here we lack even an appealing party. Directors and the dominant stockholders would, of course, not appeal; and the minority stockholders have rarely the knowledge of facts which is essential to an effective appeal, whether it be made to the directors, to the whole body of stockholders, or to the courts. Besides, the financial burden and the risks incident to any attempt of individual stockholders to interfere with an existing management is ordinarily prohibitive. Proceedings to avoid contracts with directors are, therefore, seldom brought, except after a radical change in the membership of the board. And radical changes in a board's membership are rare. Indeed the Pujo Committee reports:

"None of the witnesses (the leading American bankers testified) was able to name an instance in the history of the country in which the stockholders had succeeded in overthrowing an existing management in any large corporation. Nor does it appear that stockholders have ever even succeeded in so far as to secure the investigation of an existing management of a corporation to ascertain whether it has been well or honestly managed."

Mr. Max Pam proposed in the April, 1913, Harvard Law Review, that the government come to the aid of minority stockholders. He urged that the president of every corporation be required to report annually to the stockholders, and to state and federal officials every contract made by the company in which any director is interested; that the Attorney-General of the United States or the State investigate the same and take proper proceedings to set all such contracts aside and recover any damages suffered; or without disaffirming the contracts to recover from the interested directors the profits derived therefrom. And to this end also, that State and National Bank Examiners, State Superintendents of Insurance, and the Interstate Commerce Commission be directed to examine the records of every bank, trust company, insurance com-

pany, railroad company and every other corporation engaged in interstate commerce.   Mr. Pam's
views concerning interlocking directorates are
entitled to careful study.   As counsel promi-
nently identified with the organization of trusts,
he had for years full opportunity of weighing the
advantages and disadvantages of "Big Business."
His conviction that the practice of interlocking
directorates is a menace to the public and demands
drastic legislation, is significant.   And much can
be said in support of the specific measure which
he proposes.   But to be effective, the remedy
must be fundamental and comprehensive.

THE ESSENTIALS OF PROTECTION

Protection to minority stockholders demands
that corporations be prohibited absolutely from
making contracts in which a director has a
private interest, and that all such contracts be
declared not voidable merely, but absolutely
void.

In the case of railroads and public-service
corporations (in contradistinction to private
industrial companies), such prohibition is demanded, also, in the interests of the general
public.   For interlocking interests breed inefficiency and disloyalty; and the public pays,

in higher rates or in poor service, a large part of the penalty for graft and inefficiency. Indeed, whether rates are adequate or excessive cannot be determined until it is known whether the gross earnings of the corporation are properly expended. For when a company's important contracts are made through directors who are interested on both sides, the common presumption that money spent has been properly spent does not prevail. And this is particularly true in railroading, where the company so often lacks effective competition in its own field.

But the compelling reason for prohibiting interlocking directorates is neither the protection of stockholders, nor the protection of the public from the incidents of inefficiency and graft. Conclusive evidence (if obtainable) that the practice of interlocking directorates benefited all stockholders and was the most efficient form of organization, would not remove the objections. For even more important than efficiency are industrial and political liberty; and these are imperiled by the Money Trust. *Interlocking directorates must be prohibited, because it is impossible to break the Money Trust without putting an end to the practice in the larger corporations.*

BANKS AS PUBLIC-SERVICE CORPORATIONS

The practice of interlocking directorates is peculiarly objectionable when applied to banks, because of the nature and functions of those institutions. Bank deposits are an important part of our currency system. They are almost as essential a factor in commerce as our railways. Receiving deposits and making loans therefrom should be treated by the law not as a private business, but as one of the public services. And recognizing it to be such, the law already regulates it in many ways. The function of a bank is to receive and to loan money. It has no more right than a common carrier to use its powers specifically to build up or to destroy other businesses. The granting or withholding of a loan should be determined, so far as concerns the borrower, solely by the interest rate and the risk involved; and not by favoritism or other considerations foreign to the banking function. Men may safely be allowed to grant or to deny loans of their *own* money to whomsoever they see fit, whatsoever their motive may be. But bank resources are, in the main, not owned by the stockholders nor by the directors. Nearly three-fourths of the aggregate resources of the thirty-four banking institutions in which the Morgan associates hold a predominant influence are represented by deposits. The dependence of commerce and industry upon bank deposits, as the common reservoir of quick capital is so complete, that deposit banking should be recognized as one of the businesses "affected with a public interest." And the general rule which forbids public-service corporations from making unjust discriminations or giving undue preference should be applied to the operations of such banks.

Senator Owen, Chairman of the Committee on Banking and Currency, said recently:

"My own judgment is that a bank is a public-utility institution and cannot be treated as a private affair, for the simple reason that the public is invited, under the safeguards of the government, to deposit its money with the bank, and the public has a right to have its interests safeguarded through organized authorities. The logic of this is beyond escape. All banks in the United States, public and private, should be treated as public-utility institutions, where they receive public deposits."

The directors and officers of banking institutions must, of course, be entrusted with wide

discretion in the granting or denying of loans.
But that discretion should be exercised, not only
honestly as it affects stockholders, but also
impartially as it affects the public. Mere
honesty to the stockholders demands that the
interests to be considered by the directors be
the interests of all the stockholders; not the profit
of the part of them who happen to be its directors. But the general welfare demands of the
director, as trustee for the public, performance of
a stricter duty. The fact that the granting of
loans involves a delicate exercise of discretion
makes it difficult to determine whether the rule
of equality of treatment, which every public-
service corporation owes, has been performed.
But that difficulty merely emphasizes the importance of making absolute the rule that banks
of deposit shall not make any loan nor engage in
any transaction in which a director has a private
interest. And we should bear this in mind:
If privately-owned banks fail in the public
duty to afford borrowers equality of opportunity,
there will arise a demand for government-owned
banks, which will become irresistible.

The statement of Mr. Justice Holmes of the
Supreme Court of the United States, in the
Oklahoma Bank case, is significant:

"We cannot say that the public interests to which we have adverted, and others, are not sufficient to warrant the State in taking the whole business of banking under its control. On the contrary we are of opinion that it may go on from regulation to prohibition except upon such conditions as it may prescribe."

OFFICIAL PRECEDENTS

Nor would the requirement that banks shall make no loan in which a director has a private interest impose undue hardships or restrictions upon bank directors. It might make a bank director dispose of some of his investments and refrain from making others; but it often happens that the holding of one office precludes a man from holding another, or compels him to dispose of certain financial interests.

A judge is disqualified from sitting in any case in which he has even the smallest financial interest; and most judges, in order to be free to act in any matters arising in their court, proceed, upon taking office, to dispose of all investments which could conceivably bias their judgment in any matter that might come before them. An Interstate Commerce Commissioner is prohibited from owning any bonds or stocks in any corporation subject to the jurisdiction of the Commission. It is a serious criminal offence for any executive officer of the federal government to transact government business with any corporation in the pecuniary profits of which he is directly or indirectly interested.

And the directors of our great banking institutions, as the ultimate judges of bank credit, exercise today a function no less important to the country's welfare than that of the judges of our courts, the interstate commerce commissioners, and departmental heads.

SCOPE OF THE PROHIBITION

In the proposals for legislation on this subject, four important questions are presented:

1. Shall the principle of prohibiting interlocking directorates in potentially competing corporations be applied to state banking institutions, as well as the national banks?

2. Shall it be applied to all kinds of corporations or only to banking institutions?

3. Shall the principle of prohibiting corporations from entering into transactions in which the management has a private interest be applied to both directors and officers or be confined in its application to officers only?

4. Shall the principle be applied so as to prohibit transactions with another corporation in which one of its directors is interested merely as a stockholder?

CHAPTER IV

SERVE ONE MASTER ONLY

The Pujo Committee has presented the facts concerning the Money Trust so clearly that the conclusions appear inevitable. Their diagnosis discloses intense financial concentration and the means by which it is effected. Combination,—the intertwining of interests,—is shown to be the all-pervading vice of the present system. With a view to freeing industry, the Committee recommends the enactment of twenty-one specific remedial provisions. Most of these measures are wisely framed to meet some abuse disclosed by the evidence; and if all of these were adopted the Pujo legislation would undoubtedly alleviate present suffering and aid in arresting the disease. But many of the remedies proposed are "local" ones; and a cure is not possible, without treatment which is fundamental. Indeed, a major operation is necessary. This the Committee has hesitated to advise; although the fundamental treatment required is simple: "Serve one Master only."

The evils incident to interlocking directorates are, of course, fully recognized; but the
prohibitions proposed in that respect are restricted to a very narrow sphere.

First: The Committee recognizes that potentially competing corporations should not
have a common director;—but it restricts this
prohibition to directors of national banks,
saying:

"No officer or director of a national bank
shall be an officer or director of any other bank
or of any trust company or other financial or
other corporation or institution, whether organized under state or federal law, that is authorized to receive money on deposit or that is engaged
in the business of loaning money on collateral or
in buying and selling securities except as in this
section provided; and no person shall be an
officer or director of any national bank who is
a private banker or a member of a firm or partnership of bankers that is engaged in the business of
receiving deposits: Provided, That such bank,
trust company, financial institution, banker, or
firm of bankers is located at or engaged in business at or in the same city, town, or village as
that in which such national bank is located or
engaged in business: Provided further, That a

director of a national bank or a partner of such director may be an officer or director of not more than one trust company organized by the laws of the state in which such national bank is engaged in business and doing business at the same place."

Second: The Committee recognizes that a corporation should not make a contract in which one of the management has a private interest; but it restricts this prohibition (1) to national banks, and (2) to the officers, saying:

"No national bank shall lend or advance money or credit or purchase or discount any promissory note, draft, bill of exchange or other evidence of debt bearing the signature or indorsement of any of its officers or of any partnership of which such officer is a member, directly or indirectly, or of any corporation in which such officer owns or has a beneficial interest of upward of ten per centum of the capital stock, or lend or advance money or credit to, for or on behalf of any such officer or of any such partnership or corporation, or purchase any security from any such officer or of or from any partnership or corporation of which such officer is a member or in which he is financially interested, as herein specified, or of any corporation of which any of its officers is an officer at the time of such transaction."

Prohibitions of intertwining relations so restricted, however supplemented by other provisions, will not end financial concentration. The Money Trust snake will, at most, be scotched, not killed. The prohibition of a common director in potentially competing corporations should apply to state banks and trust companies, as well as to national banks; and it should apply to railroad and industrial corporations as fully as to banking institutions. The prohibition of corporate contracts in which one of the management has a private interest should apply to directors, as well as to officers, and to state banks and trust companies and to other classes of corporations, as well as to national banks.   And, as will be hereafter shown, such broad legislation is within the power of Congress.

Let us examine this further:

THE PROHIBITION OF COMMON DIRECTORS IN POTENTIALLY COMPETING CORPORATIONS

1. *National Banks.*   The objection to common directors, as applied to banking institutions, is clearly shown by the Pujo Committee.

"As the first and foremost step in applying a remedy, and also for reasons that seem to us conclusive, independently of that consideration, we recommend that interlocking directorates in potentially competing financial institutions be abolished and prohibited so far as lies in the power of Congress to bring about that result. . . . When we find, as in a number of instances, the same man a director in half a dozen or more banks and trust companies all located in the same section of the same city, doing the same class of business and with a like set of associates similarly situated, all belonging to the same group and representing the same class of interests, all further pretense of competition is useless. . . . If banks serving the same field are to be permitted to have common directors, genuine competition will be rendered impossible. Besides, this practice gives to such common directors the unfair advantage of knowing the affairs of borrowers in various banks, and thus affords endless opportunities for oppression."

This recommendation is in accordance with the legislation or practice of other countries. The Bank of England, the Bank of France, the National Bank of Belgium, and the leading banks of Scotland all exclude from their boards persons who are directors in other banks. By law, in Russia no person is allowed to be on the board of management of more than one bank.

The Committee's recommendation is also in harmony with laws enacted by the Commonwealth of Massachusetts more than a generation ago designed to curb financial concentration through the savings banks. Of the great wealth of Massachusetts a large part is represented by deposits in its savings banks. These deposits are distributed among 194 different banks, located in 131 different cities and towns. These 194 banks are separate and distinct; not only in form, but in fact. In order that the banks may not be controlled by a few financiers, the Massachusetts law provides that no executive officer or trustee (director) of any savings bank can hold any office in any other savings bank. That statute was passed in 1876. A few years ago it was supplemented by providing that none of the executive officers of a savings bank could hold a similar office in any national bank. Massachusetts attempted thus to curb the power of the individual financier; and no disadvantages are discernible. When that Act was passed the aggregate deposits in its savings banks were

$243,340,642; the number of deposit accounts 739,289; the average deposit to each person of the population $144. On November 1, 1912, the aggregate deposits were $838,635,097.85; the number of deposit accounts 2,200,917; the average deposit to each account $381.04. Massachusetts has shown that curbing the power of the few, at least in this respect, is entirely consistent with efficiency and with the prosperity of the whole people.

2. *State Banks and Trust Companies.* The reason for prohibiting common directors in banking institutions applies equally to national banks and to state banks including those trust companies which are essentially banks. In New York City there are 37 trust companies of which only 15 are members of the clearing house; but those 15 had on November 2, 1912, aggregate resources of $827,875,653. Indeed the Bankers' Trust Company with resources of $205,000,000, and the Guaranty Trust Company, with resources of $232,000,000, are among the most useful tools of the Money Trust. No bank in the country has larger deposits than the latter; and only one bank larger deposits than the former. If common directorships were permitted in state banks or such trust companies, the

charters of leading national banks would doubtless soon be surrendered; and the institutions
would elude federal control by re-incorporating
under state laws.

The Pujo Committee has failed to apply the
prohibition of common directorships in potentially competing banking institutions rigorously even to national banks. It permits the
same man to be a director in one national bank
and one trust company doing business in the
same place. The proposed concession opens the
door to grave dangers. In the first place the
provision would permit the interlocking of any
national bank not with one trust company only,
but with as many trust companies as the bank
has directors. For while under the Pujo bill no
one can be a national bank director who is director in more than one such trust company,
there is nothing to prevent each of the directors
of a bank from becoming a director in a different trust company. The National Bank of Commerce of New York has a board of 38 directors.
There are 37 trust companies in the City of New
York. Thirty-seven of the 38 directors might
each become a director of a different New York
trust company: and thus 37 trust companies
would be interlocked with the National Bank of

Commerce, unless the other recommendation of the Pujo Committee limiting the number of directors to 13 were also adopted.

But even if the bill were amended so as to limit the possible interlocking of a bank to a single trust company, the wisdom of the concession would still be doubtful. It is true, as the Pujo Committee states, that "the business that may be transacted by" a trust company is of "a different character" from that properly transacted by a national bank. But the business actually conducted by a trust company is, at least in the East, quite similar; and the two classes of banking institutions have these vital elements in common: each is a bank of deposit, and each makes loans from its deposits. A private banker may also transact some business of a character different from that properly conducted by a bank; but by the terms of the Committee's bill a private banker engaged in the business of receiving deposits would be prevented from being a director of a national bank; and the reasons underlying that prohibition apply equally to trust companies and to private bankers.

3. *Other Corporations.* The interlocking of banking institutions is only one of the factors

which have developed the Money Trust. The
interlocking of other corporations has been an
equally important element. And the prohibition of interlocking directorates should be extended to potentially competing corporations
whatever the class; to life insurance companies,
railroads and industrial companies, as well as
banking institutions. The Pujo Committee has
shown that Mr. George F. Baker is a common
director in the six railroads which haul 80 per
cent. of all anthracite marketed and own 88
per cent. of all anthracite deposits. The Morgan associates are the *nexus* between such supposedly competing railroads as the Northern
Pacific and the Great Northern; the Southern,
the Louisville & Nashville and the Atlantic
Coast Line, and between partially competing
industrials like the Westinghouse Electric and
Manufacturing Company and the General Electric. The *nexus* between all the large potentially competing corporations must be severed,
if the Money Trust is to be broken.

PROHIBITING CORPORATE CONTRACTS IN WHICH THE
MANAGEMENT HAS A PRIVATE INTEREST

The principle of prohibiting corporate contracts
in which the management has a private interest

is applied, in the Pujo Committee's recommendations, only to national banks, and in them only to officers. All other corporations are to be permitted to continue the practice; and even in national banks the directors are to be free to have a conflicting private interest, except that they must not accept compensation for promoting a loan of bank funds nor participate in syndicates, promotions or underwriting of securities in which their banks may be interested as underwriters or owners or lenders thereon: that all loans or other transactions in which a director is interested shall be made in his own name; and shall be authorized only after ample notice to co-directors; and that the facts shall be spread upon the records of the corporation.

The Money Trust would not be disturbed by a prohibition limited to officers. Under a law of that character, financial control would continue to be exercised by the few without substantial impairment; but the power would be exerted through a somewhat different channel. Bank officers are appointees of the directors; and ordinarily their obedient servants. Individuals who, as bank officers, are now important factors in the financial concentration, would doubtless resign as officers and become merely directors.

The loss of official salaries involved could be easily compensated. No member of the firm of J. P. Morgan & Co. is an officer in any one of the thirteen banking institutions with aggregate resources of $1,283,000,000, through which as directors they carry on their vast operations. A prohibition limited to officers would not affect the Morgan operations with these banking institutions. If there were minority representation on bank boards (which the Pujo Committee wisely advocates), such a provision might afford some protection to stockholders through the vigilance of the minority directors preventing the dominant directors using their power to the injury of the minority stockholders. But even then, the provision would not safeguard the public; and the primary purpose of Money Trust legislation is not to prevent directors from injuring stockholders; but to prevent their injuring the public through the intertwined control of the banks. No prohibition limited to officers will materially change this condition.

The prohibition of interlocking directorates, even if applied only to all banks and trust companies, would practically compel the Morgan representatives to resign from the directorates of the thirteen banking institutions with which they are connected, or from the directorates of all the railroads, express, steamship, public utility, manufacturing, and other corporations which do business with those banks and trust companies. Whether they resigned from the one or the other class of corporations, the endless chain would be broken into many pieces. And whether they retired or not, the Morgan power would obviously be greatly lessened: for if they did not retire, their field of operations would be greatly narrowed.

APPLY THE PRIVATE INTEREST PROHIBITION TO ALL KINDS OF CORPORATIONS

The creation of the Money Trust is due quite as much to the encroachment of the investment banker upon railroads, public service, industrial, and life-insurance companies, as to his control of banks and trust companies. Before the Money Trust can be broken, all these relations must be severed. And they cannot be severed unless corporations of each of these several classes are prevented from dealing with their own directors and with corporations in which those directors are interested. For instance: The most potent single source of J. P. Morgan & Co.'s power is the $162,500,000 deposits, including those of 78 interstate railroad, public-service and industrial corporations, which the Morgan firm is free to use as it sees fit. The proposed prohibition, even if applied to all banking institutions, would not affect directly this great source of Morgan power. If, however, the prohibition is made to include railroad, public-service, and industrial corporations, as well as banking institutions, members of J. P. Morgan & Co. will quickly retire from substantially all boards of directors.

APPLY THE PRIVATE INTEREST PROHIBITION TO STOCKHOLDING INTERESTS

The prohibition against one corporation entering into transactions with another corporation in which one of its directors is also interested, should apply even if his interest in the second corporation is merely that of stockholder. A conflict of interests in a director may be just as serious where he is a stockholder only in the second corporation, as if he were also a director.

One of the annoying petty monopolies, concerning which evidence was taken by the Pujo Committee, is the exclusive privilege granted to the American Bank Note Company by the New York Stock Exchange. A recent $60,000,000 issue of New York City bonds was denied listing on the Exchange, because the city refused to submit to an exaction of $55,800 by the American Company for engraving the bonds, when the New York Bank Note Company would do the work equally well for $44,500. As tending to explain this extraordinary monopoly, it was shown that men prominent in the financial world were stockholders in the American Company. Among the largest stockholders was Mr. Morgan, with 6,000 shares. No member of the Morgan firm was a director of the American Company; but there was sufficient influence exerted somehow to give the American Company the stock exchange monopoly.

The Pujo Committee, while failing to recommend that transactions in which a director has a private interest be prohibited, recognizes that a stockholder's interest of more than a certain size may be as potent an instrument of influence as a direct personal interest; for it recommends that:

"Borrowings, directly or indirectly by . . . any corporation of the stock of which he (a bank director) holds upwards of 10 per cent. from the bank of which he is such director, should only be permitted, on condition that notice shall have been given to his co-directors and that a full statement of the transaction shall be entered upon the minutes of the meeting at which such loan was authorized."

As shown above, the particular provision for notice affords no protection to the public; but if it did, its application ought to be extended to lesser stock-holdings. Indeed it is difficult to fix a limit so low that financial interest will not influence action. Certainly a stockholding interest of a single director, much smaller than 10 per cent., might be most effective in inducing favors. Mr. Morgan's stockholdings in the American Bank Note Company was only three per cent. The $6,000,000 investment of J. P. Morgan & Co. in the National City Bank represented only 6 per cent. of the bank's stock; and would undoubtedly have been effective, even if it had not been supplemented by the election of his son to the board of directors.

SPECIAL DISQUALIFICATIONS

The Stanley Committee, after investigation of the Steel Trust, concluded that the evils of interlocking directorates were so serious that representatives of certain industries which are largely

dependent upon railroads should be absolutely
prohibited from serving as railroad directors,
officers or employees. It, therefore, proposed to
disqualify as railroad director, officer or employee
any person engaged in the business of manufacturing or selling railroad cars or locomotives, railroad
rail or structural steel, or in mining and selling
coal. The drastic Stanley bill, shows how great
is the desire to do away with present abuses and
to lessen the power of the Money Trust.

Directors, officers, and employees of banking
institutions should, by a similar provision, be
disqualified from acting as directors, officers or
employees of life-insurance companies. The
Armstrong investigation showed that life-insurance companies were in 1905 the most potent
factor in financial concentration. Their power
was exercised largely through the banks and
trust companies which they controlled by stock
ownership and their huge deposits. The Armstrong legislation directed life-insurance companies to sell their stocks. The Mutual Life and
the Equitable did so in part. But the Morgan
associates bought the stocks. And now, instead
of the life-insurance companies controlling the
banks and trust companies, the latter and the
bankers control the life-insurance companies.

HOW THE PROHIBITION MAY BE LIMITED

The Money Trust cannot be destroyed unless all *classes* of corporations are included in the prohibition of interlocking directors and of transactions by corporations in which the management has a private interest. But it does not follow that the prohibition must apply to *every* corporation of each class. Certain exceptions are entirely consistent with merely protecting the public against the Money Trust; although protection of minority stockholders and business ethics demand that the rule prohibiting a corporation from making contracts in which a director has a private financial interest should be universal in its application. The number of corporations in the United States Dec. 31, 1912, was 305,336. Of these only 1610 have a capital of more than $5,000,000. Few corporations (other than banks) with a capital of less than $5,000,000 could appreciably affect general credit conditions either through their own operations or their affiliations. Corporations (other than banks) with capital resources of less than $5,000,-000 might, therefore, be excluded from the scope of the statute for the present. The prohibition could also be limited so as not to apply to any industrial concern, regardless of the amount of capital and resources, doing only an intrastate business; as practically all large industrial corporations are engaged in interstate commerce. This would exclude some retail concerns and local jobbers and manufacturers not otherwise excluded from the operation of the act. Likewise banks and trust companies located in cities of less than 100,000 inhabitants might, if thought advisable, be excluded, for the present if their capital is less than $500,000, and their resources less than, say, $2,500,000. In larger cities even the smaller banking institutions should be subject to the law. Such exceptions should overcome any objection which might be raised that in some smaller cities, the prohibition of interlocking directorates would exclude from the bank directorates all the able business men of the community through fear of losing the opportunity of bank accommodations.

An exception should also be made, so as to permit interlocking directorates between a corporation and its proper subsidiaries. And the prohibition of transactions in which the management has a private interest should, of course, not apply to contracts, express or implied, for such services as are performed indiscriminately for

the whole community by railroads and public
service corporations, or for services, common to
all customers, like the ordinary service of a bank
for its depositors.

THE POWER OF CONGRESS

The question may be asked: Has Congress
the power to impose these limitations upon the
conduct of any business other than national
banks?   And if the power of Congress is so limited, will not the dominant financiers, upon the
enactment of such a law, convert their national
banks into state banks or trust companies, and
thus escape from congressional control?

The answer to both questions is clear.   Congress has ample power to impose such prohibitions
upon practically all corporations, including state
banks, trust companies and life insurance companies; and evasion may be made impossible.
While Congress has not been granted power to
regulate *directly* state banks, and trust or life
insurance companies, or railroad, public-service
and industrial corporations, except in respect to
interstate commerce, it may do so *indirectly*
by virtue either of its control of the mail privilege
or through the taxing power.

Practically no business in the United States can

be conducted without use of the mails; and Congress may in its reasonable discretion deny the use of the mail to any business which is conducted under conditions deemed by Congress to be injurious to the public welfare. Thus, Congress has no power directly to suppress lotteries; but it has indirectly suppressed them by denying, under heavy penalty, the use of the mail to lottery enterprises. Congress has no power to suppress directly business frauds; but it is constantly doing so indirectly by issuing fraud-orders denying the mail privilege. Congress has no direct power to require a newspaper to publish a list of its proprietors and the amount of its circulation, or to require it to mark paid-matter distinctly as advertising: But it has thus regulated the press, by denying the second-class mail privilege, to all publications which fail to comply with the requirements prescribed.

The taxing power has been resorted to by Congress for like purposes: Congress has no power to regulate the manufacture of matches, or the use of oleomargarine; but it has suppressed the manufacture of the "white phosphorous" match and has greatly lessened the use of oleomargarine by imposing heavy taxes upon them. Congress has no power to prohibit, or to regulate directly the issue of bank notes by state banks, but it indirectly prohibited their issue by imposing a tax of ten per cent. upon any bank note issued by a state bank.

The power of Congress over interstate commerce has been similarly utilized. Congress cannot ordinarily provide compensation for accidents to employees or undertake directly to suppress prostitution; but it has, as an incident of regulating interstate commerce, enacted the Railroad Employers' Liability law and the White Slave Law; and it has full power over the instrumentalities of commerce, like the telegraph and the telephone.

As such exercise of congressional power has been common for, at least, half a century, Congress should not hesitate now to employ it where its exercise is urgently needed. For a comprehensive prohibition of interlocking directorates is an essential condition of our attaining the New Freedom. Such a law would involve a great change in the relation of the leading banks and bankers to other businesses. But it is the very purpose of Money Trust legislation to effect a great change; and unless it does so, the power of our financial oligarchy cannot be broken.

But though the enactment of such a law is essential to the emancipation of business, it will not *alone* restore industrial liberty.   It must be supplemented by other remedial measures.

CHAPTER V

WHAT PUBLICITY CAN DO

PUBLICITY is justly commended as a remedy for
social and industrial diseases. Sunlight is said
to be the best of disinfectants; electric light the
most efficient policeman. And publicity has
already played an important part in the struggle
against the Money Trust. The Pujo Committee
has, in the disclosure of the facts concerning
financial concentration, made a most important
contribution toward attainment of the New
Freedom. The battlefield has been surveyed and
charted. The hostile forces have been located,
counted and appraised. That was a necessary
first step—and a long one—towards relief. The
provisions in the Committee's bill concerning the
incorporation of stock exchanges and the statement to be made in connection with the listing of
securities would doubtless have a beneficent effect.
But there should be a further call upon publicity
for service. That potent force must, in the impending struggle, be utilized in many ways as a
continuous remedial measure.

Combination and control of other people's money and of other people's businesses. These ·are the main factors in the development of the Money Trust. But the wealth of the investment banker is also a factor. And with the extraordinary growth of his wealth in recent years, the relative importance of wealth as a factor in financial concentration has grown steadily. It was wealth which enabled Mr. Morgan, in 1910, to pay $3,000,000 for $51,000 par value of the stock of the Equitable Life Insurance Society. His direct income from this investment was limited by law to less than one-eighth of one per cent. a year; but it gave legal control of $504,000,000, of assets. It was wealth which enabled the Morgan associates to buy from the Equitable and the Mutual Life Insurance Company the stocks in the several banking institutions, which, merged in the Bankers' Trust Company and the Guaranty Trust Company, gave them control of $357,000,000 deposits. It was wealth which enabled Mr. Morgan to acquire his shares in the First National and National City banks, worth $21,000,000, through which he cemented the triple alliance with those institutions.

Now, how has this great wealth been accumulated? Some of it was natural accretion. Some of it is due to special opportunities for investment wisely availed of. Some of it is due to the vast extent of the bankers' operations. Then power breeds wealth as wealth breeds power. But a main cause of these large fortunes is the huge tolls taken by those who control the avenues to capital and to investors. There has been exacted as toll literally "all that the traffic will bear."

EXCESSIVE BANKERS' COMMISSIONS

The Pujo Committee was unfortunately prevented by lack of time from presenting to the country the evidence covering the amounts taken by the investment bankers as promoters' fees, underwriting commissions and profits. Nothing could have demonstrated so clearly the power exercised by the bankers, as a schedule showing the aggregate of these taxes levied within recent years. It would be well worth while now to reopen the Money Trust investigation merely to collect these data. But earlier investigations have disclosed some illuminating, though sporadic facts.

The syndicate which promoted the Steel Trust,

took, as compensation for a few weeks' work, securities yielding $62,500,000 in cash; and of this, J. P. Morgan & Co. received for their services, as Syndicate Managers, $12,500,000, besides their share, as syndicate subscribers, in the remaining $50,000,000. The Morgan syndicate took for promoting the Tube Trust $20,000,000 common stock out of a total issue of $80,000,000 stock (preferred and common). Nor were monster commissions limited to trust promotions. More recently, bankers' syndicates have, in many instances, received for floating preferred stocks of recapitalized industrial concerns, one-third of all common stock issued, besides a considerable sum in cash. And for the sale of preferred stock of well established manufacturing concerns, cash commissions (or profits) of from 7 1/2 to 10 per cent. of the cash raised are often exacted. On bonds of high-class industrial concerns, bankers' commissions (or profits) of from 5 to 10 points have been common.

Nor have these heavy charges been confined to industrial concerns. Even railroad securities, supposedly of high grade, have been subjected to like burdens. At a time when the New Haven's credit was still unimpaired, J. P. Morgan & Co. took the New York, Westchester & Boston Rail-

way first mortgage bonds, guaranteed by the
New Haven at 92 1/2; and they were marketed
at 96 1/4. They took the Portland Terminal
Company bonds, guaranteed by the Maine Central Railroad—a corporation of unquestionable
credit—at about 88, and these were marketed
at 92.

A large part of these underwriting commissions is taken by the great banking houses, not
for their services in selling the bonds, nor in assuming risks, but for securing others to sell the
bonds and incur risks. Thus when the Inter-
boro Railway—a most prosperous corporation
—financed its recent $170,000,000 bond issue,
J. P. Morgan & Co. received a 3 per cent. commission, that is, $5,100,000, practically for ar-
ranging that others should underwrite and sell
the bonds.

The aggregate commissions or profits so taken
by leading banking houses can only be conjec-
tured, as the full amount of their transactions
has not been disclosed, and the rate of commission or profit varies very widely. But the
Pujo Committee has supplied some interesting
data bearing upon the subject: Counting the
issues of securities of interstate corporations
only, J. P. Morgan & Co. directly procured the

public marketing alone or in conjunction with others during the years 1902–1912, of $1,950,-000,000. What the average commission or profit taken by J. P. Morgan & Co. was we do not know; but we do know that every one per cent. on that sum yields $19,500,000. Yet even that huge aggregate of $1,950,000,000 includes only a part of the securities on which commissions or profits were paid. It does not include any issue of an intrastate corporation. It does not include any securities privately marketed. It does not include any government, state or municipal bonds.

It is to exactions such as these that the wealth of the investment banker is in large part due. And since this wealth is an important factor in the creation of the power exercised by the Money Trust, we must endeavor to put an end to this improper wealth getting, as well as to improper combination. The Money Trust is so powerful and so firmly entrenched, that each of the sources of its undue power must be effectually stopped, if we would attain the New Freedom.

HOW SHALL EXCESSIVE CHARGES BE STOPPED?

The Pujo Committee recommends, as a remedy for such excessive charges, that interstate corporations be prohibited from entering into any

agreements creating a sole fiscal agent to dispose
of their security issues; that the issue of the
securities of interstate railroads be placed under
the supervision of the Interstate Commerce
Commission; and that their securities should be
disposed of only upon public or private competitive bids, or under regulations to be prescribed
by the Commission with full powers of investigation that will discover and punish combinations which prevent competition in bidding.
Some of the state public-service commissions
now exercise such power; and it may possibly
be wise to confer this power upon the interstate
commission, although the recommendation of the
Hadley Railroad Securities Commission are to
the contrary.   But the official regulation as proposed by the Pujo Committee would be confined
to railroad corporations; and the new security
issues of other corporations listed on the New
York Stock Exchange have aggregated in the
last five years $4,525,404,025, which is more than
either the railroad or the municipal issues.
Publicity offers, however, another and even more
promising remedy: a method of regulating
bankers' charges which would apply automatically to railroad, public-service and industrial
corporations alike.

The question may be asked: Why have these excessive charges been submitted to? Corporations, which in the first instance bear the charges for capital, have, doubtless, submitted because of banker-control; exercised directly through interlocking directorates, or kindred relations, and indirectly through combinations among bankers to suppress competition. But why have the investors submitted, since ultimately all these charges are borne by the investors, except so far as corporations succeed in shifting the burden upon the community? The large army of small investors, constituting a substantial majority of all security buyers, are entirely free from banker control. Their submission is undoubtedly due, in part, to the fact that the bankers control the avenues to recognizedly safe investments almost as fully as they do the avenues to capital. But the investor's servility is due partly, also, to his ignorance of the facts. Is it not probable that, if each investor knew the extent to which the security he buys from the banker is diluted by excessive underwritings, commissions and profits, there would be a strike of capital against these unjust exactions?

A recent British experience supports this view. In a brief period last spring nine different issues, aggregating $135,840,000, were offered by syndicates on the London market, and on the average only about 10 per cent. of these loans was taken by the public. Money was "tight," but the rates of interest offered were very liberal, and no one doubted that the investors were well supplied with funds. *The London Daily Mail* presented an explanation:

"The long series of rebuffs to new loans at the hands of investors reached a climax in the ill success of the great Rothschild issue. It will remain a topic of financial discussion for many days, and many in the city are expressing the opinion that it may have a revolutionary effect upon the present system of loan issuing and underwriting. The question being discussed is that the public have become loth to subscribe for stock which they believe the underwriters can afford, by reason of the commission they receive, to sell subsequently at a lower price than the issue price, and that the Stock Exchange has begun to realize the public's attitude. The public

sees in the underwriter not so much one who insures that the loan shall be subscribed in return
for its commission as a middleman, who, as it
were, has an opportunity of obtaining stock at
a lower price than the public in order that he
may pass it off at a profit subsequently. They
prefer not to subscribe, but to await an opportunity of dividing that profit. They feel that
if, when these issues were made, the stock were
offered them at a more attractive price, there
would be less need to pay the underwriters so
high commissions. It is another practical protest, if indirect, against the existence of the
middleman, which protest is one of the features
of present-day finance."

PUBLICITY AS A REMEDY

Compel bankers when issuing securities to
make public the commissions or profits they are
receiving. Let every circular letter, prospectus
or advertisement of a bond or stock show clearly
what the banker received for his middleman-
services, and what the bonds and stocks net
the issuing corporation. That is knowledge to
which both the existing security holder and the
prospective purchaser is fairly entitled. If the
bankers' compensation is reasonable, consider-

ing the skill and risk involved, there can be no
objection to making it known. If it is not
reasonable, the investor will "strike," as investors seem to have done recently in England.

Such disclosures of bankers' commissions or
profits is demanded also for another reason: It
will aid the investor in judging of the safety of
the investment. In the marketing of securities
there are two classes of risks: One is the risk
whether the banker (or the corporation) will find
ready purchasers for the bonds or stock at the
issue price; the other whether the investor will
get a good article. The maker of the security
and the banker are interested chiefly in getting it
sold at the issue price. The investor is interested
chiefly in buying a good article. The small
investor relies almost exclusively upon the banker
for his knowledge and judgment as to the quality
of the security; and it is this which makes his
relation to the banker one of confidence. But
at present, the investment banker occupies a
position inconsistent with that relation. The
bankers' compensation should, of course, vary
according to the risk *he* assumes. Where there
is a large risk that the bonds or stock will not be
promptly sold at the issue price, the underwriting
commission (that is the insurance premium)

should be correspondingly large. But the banker ought not to be paid more for getting *investors* to assume a larger risk. In practice the banker gets the higher commission for underwriting the weaker security, on the ground that his own risk is greater. And the weaker the security, the greater is the banker's incentive to induce his customers to relieve him. Now the law should not undertake (except incidentally in connection with railroads and public-service corporations) to fix bankers' profits. And it should not seek to prevent investors from making bad bargains. But it is now recognized in the simplest merchandising, that there should be full disclosures. The archaic doctrine of *caveat emptor* is vanishing. The law has begun to require publicity in aid of fair dealing. The Federal Pure Food Law does not guarantee quality or prices; but it helps the buyer to judge of quality by requiring disclosure of ingredients. Among the most important facts to be learned for determining the real value of a security is the amount of water it contains. And any excessive amount paid to the banker for marketing a security is water. Require a full disclosure to the investor of the amount of commissions and profits paid; and not only will investors be put on their guard, but bankers' compensation will tend to adjust itself automatically to what is fair and reasonable. Excessive commissions—this form of unjustly acquired wealth—will in large part cease.

REAL DISCLOSURE

But the disclosure must be real. And it must be a disclosure to the investor. It will not suffice to require merely the filing of a statement of facts with the Commissioner of Corporations or with a score of other officials, federal and state. That would be almost as ineffective as if the Pure Food Law required a manufacturer merely to deposit with the Department a statement of ingredients, instead of requiring the label to tell the story. Nor would the filing of a full statement with the Stock Exchange, if incorporated, as provided by the Pujo Committee bill, be adequate.

To be effective, knowledge of the facts must be actually brought home to the investor, and this can best be done by requiring the facts to be stated in good, large type in every notice, circular, letter and advertisement inviting the investor to purchase. Compliance with this requirement should also be obligatory, and not something which the investor could waive. For the whole public is interested in putting an end to the bankers' exactions. England undertook, years ago, to protect its investors against the wiles of promoters, by requiring a somewhat similar disclosure; but the British act failed, in large measure of its purpose, partly because under it the statement of facts was filed only with a public official, and partly because the investor could waive the provision. And the British statute has now been changed in the latter respect.

DISCLOSE SYNDICATE PARTICULARS

The required publicity should also include a disclosure of all participants in an underwriting. It is a common incident of underwriting that no member of the syndicate shall sell at less than the syndicate price for a definite period, unless the syndicate is sooner dissolved. In other words, the bankers make, by agreement, an artificial price. Often the agreement is probably illegal under the Sherman Anti-Trust Law. This price maintenance is, however, not necessarily objectionable. It may be entirely consistent with the general welfare, if the facts are made known. But disclosure should include a list of those participating in the underwriting so that the public may not be misled. The investor should know whether his adviser is disinterested.

Not long ago a member of a leading banking house was undertaking to justify a commission taken by his firm for floating a now favorite preferred stock of a manufacturing concern. The bankers took for their services $250,000 in cash, besides one-third of the common stock, amounting to about $2,000,000. "Of course," he said, "that would have been too much if we could have kept it all for ourselves; but we couldn't. We had to divide up a large part. There were fifty-seven participants. Why, we had even to give $10,000 of stock to————(naming the president of a leading bank in the city where the business was located). He might some day have been asked what he thought of the stock. If he had shrugged his shoulders and said he didn't know, we might have lost many a customer for the stock. We had to give him $10,000 of the stock to teach him not to shrug his shoulders."

Think of the effectiveness with practical Americans of a statement like this:

A. B. & Co.

Investment Bankers

We have today secured substantial control of the successful machinery business heretofore conducted by ——— at ——— , Illinois, which has been incorporated under the name of the Excelsior Manufacturing Company with a capital of $10,000,000, of which $5,000,000 is Preferred and $5,000,000 Common.

As we have a large clientele of confiding customers, we were able to secure from the owners an agreement for marketing the Preferred stock—we to fix a price which shall net the owners in cash $95 a share.

We offer this excellent stock to you at $100.75 per share. Our own commission or profit will be only a little over $5.00 per share, or say, $250,000 cash, besides $1,500,000 of the Common stock, which we received as a bonus. This cash and stock commission we are to divide in various proportions with the following participants in the underwriting syndicate:

C. D. & Co., New York

E. F. & Co., Boston

L. M. & Co., Philadelphia

I. K. & Co., New York.

O. P. & Co., Chicago

Were such notices common, the investment bankers would "be worthy of their hire," for only reasonable compensation would ordinarily be taken.

For marketing the preferred stock, as in the case of Excelsior Manufacturing Co. referred to above, investment bankers were doubtless essential, and as middlemen they performed a useful service. But they used their strong position to make an excessive charge. There are, however, many cases where the banker's services can be altogether dispensed with; and where that is possible he should be eliminated, not only for economy's sake, but to break up financial concentration.

CHAPTER VI

WHERE THE BANKER IS SUPERFLUOUS

THE abolition of interlocking directorates will greatly curtail the bankers' power by putting an end to many improper combinations. Publicity concerning bankers' commissions, profits and associates, will lend effective aid, particularly by curbing undue exactions. Many of the specific measures recommended by the Pujo Committee (some of them dealing with technical details) will go far toward correcting corporate and banking abuses; and thus tend to arrest financial concentration. But the investment banker has, within his legitimate province, acquired control so extensive as to menace the public welfare, even where his business is properly conducted. If the New Freedom is to be attained, every proper means of lessening that power must be availed of. A simple and effective remedy, which can be widely applied, even without new legislation, lies near at hand:—Eliminate the banker-middleman where he is superfluous.

Today practically all governments. states and

municipalities pay toll to the banker on all
bonds sold. Why should they? It is not because the banker is always needed. It is because
the banker controls the only avenue through
which the investor in bonds and stocks can ordinarily be reached. The banker has become the
universal tax gatherer. True, the *pro rata*
of taxes levied by him upon our state and city
governments is less than that levied by him upon
the corporations. But few states or cities escape
payment of some such tax to the banker on every
loan it makes. Even where the new issues of
bonds are sold at public auction, or to the highest
bidder on sealed proposals, the bankers' syndicates
usually secure large blocks of the bonds which
are sold to the people at a considerable profit.
The middleman, even though unnecessary, col-
lects his tribute.

There is a legitimate field for dealers in state
and municipal bonds, as for other merchants.
Investors already owning such bonds must have
a medium through which they can sell their
holdings. And those states or municipalities
which lack an established reputation among
investors, or which must seek more distant
markets, need the banker to distribute new issues.
But there are many states and cities which have

an established reputation and have a home market at hand. These should sell their bonds direct to investors without the intervention of a middleman. And as like conditions prevail with some corporations, their bonds and stocks should also be sold direct to the investor. Both financial efficiency and industrial liberty demand that the bankers' toll be abolished, where that is possible.

BANKER AND BROKER

The business of the investment banker must not be confused with that of the bond and stock broker. The two are often combined; but the functions are essentially different. The broker performs a very limited service. He has properly nothing to do with the original issue of securities, nor with their introduction into the market. He merely negotiates a purchase or sale as agent for another under specific orders. He exercises no discretion, except in the method of bringing buyer and seller together, or of executing orders. For his humble service he receives a moderate compensation, a commission, usually one-eighth of one per cent. (12 1/2 cents for each $100) on the par value of the security sold. The investment banker also is a mere middleman. But he is a principal, not an agent. He is also a merchant in bonds and stocks. The compensation received for his part in the transaction is in many cases more accurately described as profit than as commission. So far as concerns new issues of government, state and municipal bonds, especially, he acts as merchant, buying and selling securities on his own behalf; buying commonly at wholesale from the maker and selling at retail to the investors; taking the merchant's risk and the merchant's profits. On purchases of corporate securities the profits are often very large; but even a large profit may be entirely proper; for when the banker's services are needed and are properly performed, they are of great value. On purchases of government, state and municipal securities the profit is usually smaller; but even a very small profit cannot be justified, if unnecessary.

HOW THE BANKER CAN SERVE

The banker's services include three distinct functions, and only three:

First: Specifically as expert. The investment banker has the responsibility of the ordinary retailer to sell only that merchandise which is good of its kind. But his responsibility in this respect is unusually heavy, because he deals in an article on which a great majority of his customers are unable, themselves, to pass intelligent judgment without aid.   The purchase by the investor of most corporate securities is little better than a gamble, where he fails to get the advice of some one who has investigated the security thoroughly as the banker should.   For few investors have the time, the facilities, or the ability to investigate properly the value of corporate securities.

Second: Specifically as distributor. The banker performs an all-important service in providing an outlet for securities.   His connections enable him to reach possible buyers quickly.   And goodwill—that is, possession of the confidence of regular customers—enables him to effect sales where the maker of the security might utterly fail to find a market.

Third: Specifically as jobber or retailer.   The investment banker, like other merchants, carries his stock in trade until it can be marketed.   In this he performs a service which is often of great value to the maker.   Needed cash is obtained immediately, because the whole issue of securities can thus be disposed of by a single transaction. And even where there is not immediate payment, the knowledge that the money will be provided when needed is often of paramount importance.

By carrying securities in stock, the banker performs a service also to investors, who are thereby enabled to buy securities at such times as they desire.

Whenever makers of securities or investors require all or any of these three services, the investment banker is needed, and payment of compensation to him is proper. Where there is no such need, the banker is clearly superfluous. And in respect to the original issue of many of our state and municipal bonds, and of some corporate securities, no such need exists.

WHERE THE BANKER SERVES NOT

It needs no banker experts in value to tell us that bonds of Massachusetts or New York, of Boston, Philadelphia or Baltimore and of scores of lesser American cities, are safe investments. The basic financial facts in regard to such bonds are a part of the common knowledge of many American investors; and, certainly, of most possible investors who reside in the particular state or city whose bonds are in question. Where the financial facts are not generally known, they are so simple, that they can be easily summarized and understood by any prospective investor without interpretation by an expert. Bankers often employ, before purchasing securities, their own accountants to verify the statements supplied by the makers of the security, and use these account-ants' certificates as an aid in selling. States and municipalities, the makers of the securities, might for the same purpose employ independent public accountants of high reputation, who would give their certificates for use in marketing the securities. Investors could also be assured with-out banker-aid that the basic legal conditions are sound. Bankers, before purchasing an issue of securities, customarily obtain from their own counsel an opinion as to its legality, which inves-tors are invited to examine. It would answer the same purpose, if states and municipalities should supplement the opinion of their legal representatives by that of independent counsel of recognized professional standing, who would certify to the legality of the issue.

Neither should an investment banker be needed to find investors willing to take up, in small lots, a new issue of bonds of New York or Massa-chusetts, of Boston, Philadelphia or Baltimore, or a hundred other American cities. A state or municipality seeking to market direct to the investor its own bonds would naturally experi-ence, at the outset, some difficulty in marketing a

large issue.   And in a newer community, where
there is little accumulation of unemployed capital,
it might be impossible to find buyers for any large
issue.   Investors are apt to be conservative;
and they have been trained to regard the intervention of the banker as necessary.   The bankers
would naturally discourage any attempt of states
and cities to dispense with their services.   Entrance upon a market, hitherto monopolized by
them, would usually have to be struggled for.
But banker-fed investors, as well as others could,
in time, be brought to realize the advantage of
avoiding the middleman and dealing directly with
responsible borrowers.   Governments, like private
concerns, would have to do educational work; but
this publicity would be much less expensive and
much more productive than that undertaken by
the bankers.   Many investors are already impa-
tient of banker exactions; and eager to deal
directly with governmental agencies in whom they
have more confidence.   And a great demand could,
at once, be developed among smaller investors
whom the bankers have been unable to interest,
and who now never buy state or municipal bonds.
The opening of this new field would furnish a market, in some respects more desirable and certainly
wider than that now reached by the bankers.

Neither do states or cities ordinarily need the services of the investment banker to carry their bonds pending distribution to the investor. Where there is immediate need for large funds, states and cities—at least the older communities —should be able to raise the money temporarily, quite as well as the bankers do now, while awaiting distribution of their bonds to the investor. Bankers carry the bonds with other people's money, not with their own. Why should not cities get the temporary use of other people's money as well? Bankers have the preferential use of the deposits in the banks, often because they control the banks. Free these institutions from banker-control, and no applicant to borrow the people's money will be received with greater favor than our large cities. Boston, with its $1,500,000,000 of assessed valuation and $78,033,-128 net debt, is certainly as good a risk as even Lee, Higginson & Co. or Kidder, Peabody & Co.

But ordinarily cities do not, or should not, require large sums of money at any one time. Such need of large sums does not arise except from time to time where maturing loans are to be met, or when some existing public utility plant is to be taken over from private owners. Large issues of bonds for any other purpose are usually made in anticipation of future needs, rather than to meet present necessities. Modern efficient public financiering, through substituting serial bonds for the long term issues (which in Massachusetts has been made obligatory) will, in time, remove the need of large sums at one time for paying maturing debts, since each year's maturities will be paid from the year's taxes. Purchases of existing public utility plants are of rare occurrence, and are apt to be preceded by long periods of negotiation. When they occur they can, if foresight be exercised, usually be financed without full cash payment at one time.

Today, when a large issue of bonds is made, the banker, while ostensibly paying his own money to the city, actually pays to the city other people's money which he has borrowed from the banks. Then the banks get back, through the city's deposits, a large part of the money so received. And when the money is returned to the bank, the banker has the opportunity of borrowing it again for other operations. The process results in double loss to the city. The city loses by not getting from the banks as much for its bonds as investors would pay. And then it loses interest on the money raised before it is needed. For the bankers receive from the city bonds bearing rarely

less than 4 per cent. interest; while the proceeds
are deposited in the banks which rarely allow
more than 2 per cent. interest on the daily
balances.

CITIES THAT HELPED THEMSELVES

In the present year some cities have been led by
necessity to help themselves. The bond market
was poor. Business was uncertain, money tight
and the ordinary investor reluctant. Bankers
were loth to take new bond issues. Municipalities were unwilling to pay the high rates demanded of them. And many cities were prohibited by law or ordinance from paying more than
4 per cent. interest; while good municipal bonds
were then selling on a 4 1/2 to 5 per cent. basis.
But money had to be raised, and the attempt was
made to borrow it direct from the lenders instead
of from the banker-middleman. Among the
cities which raised money in this way were Philadelphia, Baltimore, St. Paul, and Utica, New
York.

Philadelphia, under Mayor Blankenburg's
inspiration, sold nearly $4,175,000 in about two
days on a 4 per cent. basis and another "over-the-
counter" sale has been made since. In Baltimore, with the assistance of the *Sun*, $4,766,000

were sold "over the counter" on a 4 1/2 per cent.
basis. Utica's two "popular sales" of 4 1/2
per cent. bonds were largely "over-subscribed."
And since then other cities large and small
have had their "over-the-counter" bond sales.
The experience of Utica, as stated by its Controller, Fred G. Reusswig, must prove of general
interest:

"In June of the present year I advertised for
sale two issues, one of $100,000, and the other of
$19,000, bearing interest at 4 1/2 per cent. The
latter issue was purchased at par by a local bidder
and of the former we purchased $10,000 for our
sinking funds. That left $90,000 unsold, for
which there were no bidders, which was the first
time that I had been unable to sell our bonds.
About this time the 'popular sales' of Baltimore
and Philadelphia attracted my attention. The
laws in effect in those cities did not restrict the
officials as does our law and I could not copy their
methods. I realized that there was plenty of
money in this immediate vicinity and if I could
devise a plan conforming with our laws under
which I could make the sale attractive to small
investors it would undoubtedly prove successful.
I had found, in previous efforts to interest people
of small means, that they did not understand the

meaning of premium and would rather not buy than bid above par. They also objected to making a deposit with their bids. In arranging for the 'popular sales' I announced in the papers that, while I must award to the highest bidder, it was my opinion that a par bid would be *the highest bid*. I also announced that we would issue bonds in denominations as low as $100 and that we would not require a deposit except where the bid was $5,000 or over. Then I succeeded in getting the local papers to print editorials and local notices upon the subject of municipal bonds, with particular reference to those of Utica and the forthcoming sale. All the prospective purchaser had to do was to fill in the amount desired, sign his name, seal the bid and await the day for the award. I did not have many bidders for very small amounts. There was only one for $100 at the first sale and one for $100 at the second sale and not more than ten who wanted less than $500. Most of the bidders were looking for from $1,000 to $5,000, but nearly all were people of comparatively small means, and with some the investment represented all their savings. In awarding the bonds I gave preference to residents of Utica and I had no difficulty in apportioning the various maturities in a satisfactory way.

"I believe that there are a large number of persons in every city who would buy their own bonds if the way were made easier by law. Syracuse and the neighboring village of Ilion, both of which had been unable to sell in the usual way, came to me for a program of procedure and both have since had successful sales along similar lines. We have been able by this means to keep the interest rate on our bonds at 4 1/2 per cent., while cities which have followed the old plan of relying upon bond houses have had to increase the rate to 5 per cent. I am in favor of amending the law in such a manner that the Common Council, approved by the Board of Estimate and Apportionment, may fix the prices at which bonds shall be sold, instead of calling for competitive bids. Then place the bonds on sale at the Controller's office to any one who will pay the price. The prices upon each issue should be graded according to the different values of different maturities. Under the present law, as we have it, conditions are too complicated to make a sale practicable except upon a basis of par bids."

THE ST. PAUL EXPERIMENT

St. Paul wisely introduced into its experiment a more democratic feature, which Tom L. Johnson,

Cleveland's great mayor, thought out (but did not utilize), and which his friend W. B. Colver, now Editor-in-Chief of the *Daily News*, brought to the attention of the St. Paul officials.   Mayor Johnson had recognized the importance of reaching the small savings of the people; and concluded that it was necessary not only to issue the bonds in very small denominations, but also to make them redeemable at par.   He sought to combine practically, bond investment with the savings bank privilege.   The fact that municipal bonds are issuable ordinarily only in large denominations, say, $1,000, presented an obstacle to be overcome.   Mayor Johnson's plan was to have the sinking fund commissioners take large blocks of the bonds, issue against them certificates in denominations of $10, and have the commissioners agree (under their power to purchase securities) to buy the certificates back at par and interest.   Savings bank experience, he insisted, showed that the redemption feature would not prove an embarrassment; as the percentage of those wishing to withdraw their money is small; and deposits are nearly always far in excess of withdrawals.

The St. Paul sinking fund commissioners and City Attorney O'Neill approved the Johnson plan; and in the face of high money rates, sold on a 4 per cent. basis, during July, certificates to the net amount of $502,300; during August, $147,-000; and during September, over $150,000, the average net sales being about $5,700 a day. Mr. Colver, reporting on the St. Paul experience, said:

"There have been about 2,000 individual purchasers making the average deposit about $350 or $360. There have been no certificates sold to banks. During the first month the deposits averaged considerably higher and for this reason: in very many cases people who had savings which represented · the accumulation of considerable time, withdrew their money from the postal savings banks, from the regular banks, from various hiding places and deposited them with the city. Now these same people are coming once or twice a month and making deposits of ten or twenty dollars, so that the average of the individual deposit has fallen very rapidly during September and every indication is that the number of small deposits will continue to increase and the relatively large deposits become less frequent as time goes on.

As a matter of fact, these certificate deposits are stable, far more than the deposits and investments of richer people who watch for advantageous reinvestments and who shift their money about rather freely. The man with three or four hundred dollars savings will suffer almost anything before he will disturb that fund. We believe that the deposits every day here, day in and day out, will continue to take care of all the withdrawals and still leave a net gain for the day, that net figure at present being about $5,700 a day."

Many cities are now prevented from selling bonds direct to the small investors, through laws which compel bonds to be issued in large denominations or which require the issue to be offered to the highest bidder. These legislative limitations should be promptly removed.

SALESMANSHIP AND EDUCATION

Such success as has already been attained is largely due to the unpaid educational work of leading progressive newspapers. But the educational work to be done must not be confined to teaching "the people"—the buyers of the bonds. Municipal officials and legislators have quite as much to learn. They must, first of all, study salesmanship. Selling bonds to the people is a

new art, still undeveloped. The general problems
have not yet been worked out. And besides
these problems common to all states and cities,
there will be, in nearly every community, local
problems which must be solved, and local difficulties which must be overcome. The proper solu-
tion even of the general problems must take considerable time. There will have to be many ex-
periments made; and doubtless there will be many
failures. Every great distributor of merchandise
knows the obstacles which he had to overcome
before success was attained; and the large sums
that had to be invested in opening and preparing
a market. Individual concerns have spent millions in wise publicity; and have ultimately reaped
immense profits when the market was won.
Cities must take their lessons from these great
distributors. Cities must be ready to study the
problems and to spend prudently for proper publicity work. It might, in the end, prove an economy, even to allow, on particular issues, where necessary, a somewhat higher interest rate than bankers would exact, if thereby a direct market for
bonds could be secured. Future operations would
yield large economies. And the obtaining of a
direct market for city bonds is growing ever more
important, because of the huge increase in loans

which must attend the constant expansion of municipal functions. In 1898 the new municipal issues aggregated $103,084,793; in 1912, $380,810,287.

SAVINGS BANKS AS CUSTOMERS

In New York, Massachusetts and the other sixteen states where a system of purely mutual savings banks is general, it is possible, with a little organization, to develop an important market for the direct purchaser of bonds. The bonds issued by Massachusetts cities and towns have averaged recently about $15,000,000 a year, and those of the state about $3,000,000. The 194 Massachusetts savings banks, with aggregate assets of $902,105,755.94, held on October 31, 1912, $90,536,581.32 in bonds and notes of states and municipalities. Of this sum about $60,000,-000 are invested in bonds and notes of Massachusetts cities and towns, and about $8,000,000 in state issues. The deposits in the savings banks are increasing at the rate of over $30,000,000 a year. Massachusetts state and municipal bonds have, within a few years, come to be issued tax exempt in the hands of the holder, whereas other classes of bonds usually held by savings banks are subject to a tax of one-half of one per cent.

of the market value. Massachusetts savings
banks, therefore, will to an increasing extent, select Massachusetts municipal issues for high-grade
bond investments. Certainly Massachusetts cities and towns might, with the coöperation of the
Commonwealth, easily develop a "home market"
for "over-the-counter" bond business with the
savings banks. And the savings banks of other
states offer similar opportunities to their municipalities.

COÖPERATION

Bankers obtained their power through combination. Why should not cities and states
by means of coöperation free themselves from
the bankers? For by coöperation between the
cities and the state, the direct marketing of
municipal bonds could be greatly facilitated.

Massachusetts has 33 cities, each with a population of over 12,000 persons; 71 towns each
with a population of over 5,000; and 250 towns
each with a population of less than 5,000. Three
hundred and eight of these municipalities now
have funded indebtedness outstanding. The
aggregate net indebtedness is about $180,000,000.
Every year about $15,000,000 of bonds and notes
are issued by the Massachusetts cities and towns

for the purpose of meeting new requirements and refunding old indebtedness. If these municipalities would coöperate in marketing securities, the market for the bonds of each municipality would be widened; and there would exist also a common market for Massachusetts municipal securities which would be usually well supplied, would receive proper publicity and would attract investors. Successful merchandising obviously involves carrying an adequate, well-assorted stock. If every city acts alone, in endeavoring to market its bonds direct, the city's bond-selling activity will necessarily be sporadic. Its ability to supply the investor will be limited by its own necessities for money. The market will also be limited to the bonds of the particular municipality. But if a state and its cities should coöperate, there could be developed a continuous and broad market for the sale of bonds "over-the-counter." The joint selling agency of over three hundred municipalities,—as in Massachusetts—would naturally have a constant supply of assorted bonds and notes which could be had in as small amounts as the investor might want to buy them. It would be a simple matter to establish such a joint selling agency by which municipalities, under proper regulation of, and aid from the state, would coöperate.

And coöperation among the cities and with the state might serve in another important respect. These 354 Massachusetts municipalities carry in the aggregate large bank balances. Sometimes the balance carried by a city represents unexpended revenues; sometimes unexpended proceeds of loans. On these balances they usually receive from the banks 2 per cent. interest. The balances of municipalities vary like those of other depositors; one having idle funds, when another is in need. Why should not all of these cities and towns coöperate, making, say, the State their common banker, and supply each other with funds as farmers and laborers coöperate through credit unions? Then cities would get, instead of 2 per cent. on their balances, all their money was worth.

The Commonwealth of Massachusetts holds now in its sinking and other funds nearly $30,000-000 of Massachusetts municipal securities, constituting nearly three-fourths of all securities held in these funds. Its annual purchases aggregate nearly $4,000,000. Its purchases direct from cities and towns have already exceeded $1,000,000 this year. It would be but a simple extension of the state's function to coöperate, as indicated, in a joint, Municipal Bond Selling Agency and Credit Union. It would be a distinct advance in the efficiency of state and municipal financing; and what is even more important, a long step toward the emancipation of the people from banker-control.

CORPORATE SELF-HELP

Strong corporations with established reputations, locally or nationally, could emancipate themselves from the banker in a similar manner. Public-service corporations in some of our leading cities could easily establish "over-the-counter" home markets for their bonds; and would be greatly aided in this by the supervision now being exercised by some state commissions over the issue of securities by such corporations. Such corporations would gain thereby not only in freedom from banker-control and exactions, but in the winning of valuable local support. The investor's money would be followed by his sympathy. In things economic, as well as in things political, wisdom and safety lie in direct appeals to the people.

The Pennsylvania Railroad now relies largely upon its stockholders for new capital. But a

corporation with its long-continued success and
reputation for stability should have much wider
financial support and should eliminate the banker
altogether. With the 2,700 stations on its
system, the Pennsylvania could, with a slight
expense, create nearly as many avenues through
which money would be obtainable to meet its
growing needs.

BANKER PROTECTORS

It may be urged that reputations often outlive
the conditions which justify them, that outlived
reputations are pitfalls to the investors; and that
the investment banker is needed to guard him
from such dangers. True; but when have the
big bankers or 'their little satellites protected the
people from such pitfalls?

Was there ever a more be-bankered railroad
than the New Haven? Was there ever a more
banker-led community of investors than New
England? Six years before the fall of that great
system, the hidden dangers were pointed out to
these banker-experts. Proof was furnished of
the rotting timbers. The disaster-breeding policies were laid bare. The bankers took no action.
Repeatedly, thereafter, the bankers' attention
was called to the steady deterioration of the

structure. The New Haven books disclose 11,-
481 stockholders who are residents of Massachusetts; 5,682 stockholders in Connecticut; 735
in Rhode Island; and 3,510 in New York. Of
the New Haven stockholders 10,474 were women.
Of the New Haven stockholders 10,222 were of
such modest means that their holdings were from
one to ten shares only. The investors were
sorely in need of protection. The city directories
disclose 146 banking houses in Boston, 26 in
Providence, 33 in New Haven and Hartford,
and 357 in New York City. But who, connected
with those New England and New York banking houses, during the long years which preceded the recent investigation of the Interstate
Commerce Commission, raised either voice or
pen in protest against the continuous mismanage-
ment of that great trust property or warned the
public of the impending disaster? Some of the
bankers sold their own stock holdings. Some
bankers whispered to a few favored customers
advice to dispose of New Haven stock. But not
one banker joined those who sought to open the
eyes of New England to the impending disaster
and to avert it by timely measures. New
England's leading banking houses were ready to
"coöperate" with the New Haven management

in taking generous commissions for marketing the endless supply of new securities; but they did nothing to protect the investors. Were these bankers blind? Or were they afraid to oppose the will of J. P. Morgan & Co.?

Perhaps it is the banker who, most of all, needs the New Freedom.

CHAPTER VII

BIG MEN AND LITTLE BUSINESS

J. P. MORGAN & Co. declare, in their letter to the Pujo Committee, that "practically all the railroad and industrial development of this country has taken place initially through the medium of the great banking houses." That statement is entirely unfounded in fact. On the contrary nearly every such contribution to our comfort and prosperity was "initiated" *without* their aid. The "great banking houses" came into relation with these enterprises, either after success had been attained, or upon "reorganization" after the possibility of success had been demonstrated, but the funds of the hardy pioneers, who had risked their all, were exhausted.

This is true of our early railroads, of our early street railways, and of the automobile; of the telegraph, the telephone and the wireless; of gas and oil; of harvesting machinery, and of our steel industry; of the textile, paper and shoe industries; and of nearly every other important branch of manufacture. The *initiation* of each

of these enterprises may properly be character-
ized as "great transactions"; and the men who
contributed the financial aid and business management necessary for their introduction are
entitled to share, equally with inventors, in our
gratitude for what has been accomplished. But
the instances are extremely rare where the original financing of such enterprises was undertaken
by investment bankers, great or small. It was
usually done by some common business man,
accustomed to taking risks; or by some well-to-
do friend of the inventor or pioneer, who was
influenced largely by considerations other than
money-getting. Here and there you will find
that banker-aid was given; but usually in those
cases it was a small local banking concern, not
a "great banking house" which helped to "initiate" the undertaking.

RAILROADS

We have come to associate the great bankers
with railroads.   But their part was not conspicuous in the early history of the Eastern railroads;
and in the Middle West the experience was, to
some extent, similar. The Boston & Maine
Railroad owns and leases 2,215 miles of line; but
it is a composite of about 166 separate railroad

companies. The New Haven Railroad owns
and leases 1,996 miles of line; but it is a composite of 112 separate railroad companies. The
necessary capital to build these little roads was
gathered together, partly through state, county
or municipal aid; partly from business men or
landholders who sought to advance their special
interests; partly from investors; and partly from
well-to-do public-spirited men, who wished to
promote the welfare of their particular communities. About seventy-five years after the first of
these railroads was built, J. P. Morgan & Co.
became fiscal agent for all of them by creating the
New Haven-Boston & Maine monopoly.

STEAMSHIPS

The history of our steamship lines is similar.
In 1807, Robert Fulton, with the financial aid of
Robert R. Livingston, a judge and statesman—not
a banker—demonstrated with the *Claremont*,
that it was practicable to propel boats by steam.
In 1833 the three Cunard brothers of Halifax
and 232 other persons—stockholders of the
Quebec and Halifax Steam Navigation Company—joined in supplying about $80,000 to
build the *Royal William*,—the first steamer to
cross the Atlantic. In 1902, many years after

individual enterprises had developed practically all the great ocean lines, J. P. Morgan & Co. floated the International Mercantile Marine with its $52,744,000 of 4 1/2 bonds, now selling at about 60, and $100,000,000 of stock (preferred and common) on which no dividend has ever been paid.   It was just sixty-two years after the first regular line of transatlantic steamers— The Cunard—was founded that Mr. Morgan organized the Shipping Trust.

TELEGRAPH

The story of the telegraph is similar.   The money for developing Morse's invention was supplied by his partner and co-worker, Alfred Vail.   The initial line (from Washington to Baltimore) was built with an appropriation of $30,000 made by Congress in 1843.   Sixty-six years later J. P. Morgan & Co. became bankers for the Western Union through financing its purchase by the American Telephone & Telegraph Company.

HARVESTING MACHINERY

Next to railroads and steamships, harvesting machinery has probably been the most potent factor in the development of America; and most important of the harvesting machines was Cyrus H. McCormick's reaper. That made it possible to increase the grain harvest twenty- or thirty-fold. No investment banker had any part in introducing this great business man's invention.

McCormick was without means; but William Butler Ogden, a railroad builder, ex-Mayor and leading citizen of Chicago, supplied $25,000 with which the first factory was built there in 1847. Fifty-five years later, J. P. Morgan & Co. performed the service of combining the five great harvester companies, and received a commission of $3,000,000. The concerns then consolidated as the International Harvester Company, with a capital stock of $120,000,000, had, despite their huge assets and earning power, been previously capitalized, in the aggregate, at only $10,500,000—strong evidence that in all the preceding years no investment banker had financed them. Indeed, McCormick was as able in business as in mechanical invention. Two years after Odgen paid him $25,000 for a half interest in the business, McCormick bought it back for $50,000; and thereafter, until his death in 1884, no one but members of the McCormick family had any interest in the business.

THE BANKER ERA

It may be urged that railroads and steamships, the telegraph and harvesting machinery were introduced before the accumulation of investment capital had developed the investment banker, and before America's "great banking houses" had been established; and that, consequently, it would be fairer to inquire what services bankers had rendered in connection with later industrial development. The firm of J. P. Morgan & Co. is fifty-five years old; Kuhn, Loeb & Co. fifty-six years old; Lee, Higginson & Co. over fifty years; and Kidder, Peabody & Co. forty-eight years; and yet the investment banker seems to have had almost as little part in "initiating" the great improvements of the last half century, as did bankers in the earlier period.

STEEL

The modern steel industry of America is forty-five years old. The "great bankers" had no part in initiating it. Andrew Carnegie, then already a man of large means, introduced the Bessemer process in 1868. In the next thirty years our steel and iron industry increased greatly. By 1898 we had far outstripped all competitors.

America's production about equalled the aggregate of England and Germany. We had also
reduced costs so much that Europe talked of the
"American Peril." It was 1898, when J. P.
Morgan & Co. took their first step in forming the
Steel Trust, by organizing the Federal Steel
Company. Then followed the combination of
the tube mills into an $80,000,000 corporation,
J. P. Morgan & Co. taking for their syndicate
services $20,000,000 of common stock. About
the same time the consolidation of the bridge and
structural works, the tin plate, the sheet steel, the
hoop and other mills followed; and finally, in
1901, the Steel Trust was formed, with a capitalization of $1,402,000,000. These combinations
came thirty years after the steel industry had
been "initiated".

THE TELEPHONE

The telephone industry is less than forty years
old. It is probably America's greatest contribution to industrial development. The bankers
had no part in "initiating" it. The glory belongs
to a simple, enthusiastic, warm-hearted, business
man of Haverhill, Massachusetts, who was willing
to risk *his own* money. H. N. Casson tells of
this, most interestingly, in his "History of the
Telephone":

"The only man who had money and dared to stake it on the future of the telephone was Thomas Sanders, and he did this not mainly for business reasons. Both he and Hubbard were attached to Bell primarily by sentiment, as Bell had removed the blight of dumbness from Sanders' little son, and was soon to marry Hubbard's daughter. Also, Sanders had no expectation, at first, that so much money would be needed. He was not rich. His entire business, which was that of cutting out soles for shoe manufacturers, was not at any time worth more than thirty-five thousand dollars. Yet, from 1874 to 1878, he had advanced nine-tenths of the money that was spent on the telephone. The first five thousand telephones, and more, were made with his money. And so many long, expensive months dragged by before any relief came to Sanders, that he was compelled, much against his will and his business judgment, to stretch his credit within an inch of the breaking-point to help Bell and the telephone. Desperately he signed note after note until he faced a total of one hundred and ten thousand dollars. If the new 'scientific toy' succeeded, which he often doubted, he would be the richest citizen in Haverhill; and if it failed, which he sorely feared, he would be a bankrupt.

Sanders and Hubbard were leasing telephones two
by two, to business men who previously had been
using the private lines of the Western Union
Telegraph Company. This great corporation
was at this time their natural and inevitable
enemy. It had swallowed most of its competitors, and was reaching out to monopolize all
methods of communication by wire. The rosiest
hope that shone in front of Sanders and Hubbard
was that the Western Union might conclude to
buy the Bell patents, just as it had already bought
many others. In one moment of discourage-
ment they had offered the telephone to President
Orton, of the Western Union, for $100,000; and
Orton had refused it. 'What use,' he asked
pleasantly, 'could this company make of an electrical toy?'

"But besides the operation of its own wires, the
Western Union was supplying customers with
various kinds of printing-telegraphs and dial-
telegraphs, some of which could transmit sixty
words a minute. These accurate instruments, it
believed, could never be displaced by such a scientific oddity as the telephone, and it continued to
believe this until one of its subsidiary companies
—the Gold and Stock—reported that several of
its machines had been superseded by telephones.

"At once the Western Union awoke from its indifference. Even this tiny nibbling at its business must be stopped. It took action quickly, and organized the 'American Speaking-Telephone Company,' and with $300,000 capital, and with three electrical inventors, Edison, Gray, and Dolbear, on its staff. With all the bulk of its great wealth and prestige, it swept down upon Bell and his little body-guard. It trampled upon Bell's patent with as little concern as an elephant can have when he tramples upon an ant's nest. To the complete bewilderment of Bell, it coolly announced that it had the only original telephone, and that it was ready to supply superior telephones with all the latest improvements made by the original inventors—Dolbear, Gray, and Edison.

"The result was strange and unexpected. The Bell group, instead of being driven from the field, were at once lifted to a higher level in the business world. And the Western Union, in the endeavor to protect its private lines, became involuntarily a 'bell-wether' to lead capitalists in the direction of the telephone."

Even then, when financial aid came to the Bell enterprise, it was from capitalists, not from bankers, and among these capitalists was William H.

Forbes (son of the builder of the Burlington) who became the first President of the Bell Telephone Company. That was in 1878. More than twenty years later, after the telephone had spread over the world, the great house of Morgan came into financial control of the property. The American Telephone & Telegraph Company was formed. The process of combination became active. Since January, 1900, its stock has increased from $25,886,300 to $344,606,400. In six years (1906 to 1912), the Morgan associates marketed about $300,000,000 bonds of that company or its subsidiaries. In that period the volume of business done by the telephone companies had, of course, grown greatly, and the plant had to be constantly increased; but the proceeds of these huge security issues were used, to a large extent, in effecting combinations; that is, in buying out telephone competitors; in buying control of the Western Union Telegraph Company; and in buying up outstanding stock interests in semi-independent Bell companies. It is these combinations which have led to the investigation of the Telephone Company by the Department of Justice; and they are, in large part, responsible for the movement to have the government take over the telephone business.

ELECTRICAL MACHINERY

The business of manufacturing electrical machinery and apparatus is only a little over thirty years old. J. P. Morgan & Co. became interested early in one branch of it; but their dominance of the business today is due, not to their "initiating" it, but to their effecting a combination, and organizing the General Electric Company in 1892. There were then three large electrical companies, the Thomson-Houston, the Edison and the Westinghouse, besides some small ones. The Thomson-Houston of Lynn, Massachusetts, was in many respects the leader, having been formed to introduce, among other things, important inventions of Prof. Elihu Thomson and Prof. Houston. Lynn is one of the principal shoe-manufacturing centers of America. It is within ten miles of State Street, Boston; but Thomson's early financial support came not from Boston bankers, but mainly from Lynn business men and investors; men active, energetic, and used to taking risks with *their own* money. Prominent among them was Charles A. Coffin, a shoe manufacturer, who became connected with the Thomson-Houston Company upon its organization and president of the General Electric when Mr. Morgan formed that company in 1892, by combining the Thomson-Houston and the Edison. To his continued service, supported by other Thomson-Houston men in high positions, the great prosperity of the company is, in large part, due. The two companies so combined controlled probably one-half of all electrical patents then existing in America; and certainly more than half of those which had any considerable value.

In 1896 the General Electric pooled its patents with the Westinghouse, and thus competition was further restricted. In 1903 the General Electric absorbed the Stanley Electric Company, its other large competitor; and became the largest manufacturer of electric apparatus and machinery in the world. In 1912 the resources of the Company were $131,942,144. It billed sales to the amount of $89,182,185. It employed directly over 60,000 persons,—more than a fourth as many as the Steel Trust. And it is protected against "undue" competition; for one of the Morgan partners has been a director, since 1909, in the Westinghouse,—the only other large electrical machinery company in America.

THE AUTOMOBILE

The automobile industry is about twenty years old. It is now America's most prosperous

business.   When Henry B. Joy, President of the
Packard Motor Car Company, was asked to
what extent the bankers aided in "initiating"
the automobile, he replied:

"It is the observable facts of history, it is also
my experience of thirty years as a business man,
banker, etc., that first the seer conceives an opportunity.   He has faith in his almost second sight.
He believes he can do something—develop a
business—construct an industry—build a railroad
—or Niagara Falls Power Company,—and make
it pay!

"Now the human measure is not the actual
physical construction, but the 'make it pay'!

"A man raised the money in the late '90s and
built a beet sugar factory in Michigan.   Wise-
acres said it was nonsense.   He gathered together
the money from his friends who would take a
chance with him.   He not only built the sugar
factory (and there was never any doubt of his
ability to do that) but he made it pay.   The next
year two more sugar factories were built, and
were financially successful.   These were built by
private individuals of wealth, taking chances
in the face of cries of doubting bankers and
trust companies.

"Once demonstrated that the industry was a sound one financially and *then* bankers and trust companies would lend the new sugar companies which were speedily organized a large part of the necessary funds to construct and operate.

"The motor-car business was the same.

"When a few gentlemen followed me in my vision of the possibilities of the business, the banks and older business men (who in the main were the banks) said, 'fools and their money soon to be parted'—etc., etc.

"Private capital at first establishes an industry, backs it through its troubles, and, if possible, wins financial success when banks would not lend a dollar of aid.

"The business once having proved to be practicable and financially successful, then do the banks lend aid to its needs."

Such also was the experience of the greatest of the many financial successes in the automobile industry—the Ford Motor Company.

HOW BANKERS ARREST DEVELOPMENT

But "great banking houses" have not merely failed to initiate industrial development; they have definitely arrested development because to them the creation of the trusts is largely due. The recital in the Memorial addressed to the President by the Investors' Guild in November, 1911, is significant:

"It is a well-known fact that modern trade combinations tend strongly toward constancy of process and products, and by their very nature are opposed to new processes and new products originated by independent inventors, and hence tend to restrain competition in the development and sale of patents and patent rights; and consequently tend to discourage independent inventive thought, to the great detriment of the nation, and with injustice to inventors whom the Constitution especially intended to encourage and protect in their rights."

And more specific was the testimony of the *Engineering News:*

"We are today something like five years behind Germany in iron and steel metallurgy, and such innovations as are being introduced by our iron and steel manufacturers are most of them merely following the lead set by foreigners years ago.

"We do not believe this is because American

engineers are any less ingenious or original than those of Europe, though they may indeed be deficient in training and scientific education compared with those of Germany. We believe the main cause is the wholesale consolidation which has taken place in American industry. A huge organization is too clumsy to take up the development of an original idea. With the market closely controlled and profits certain by following standard methods, those who control our trusts do not want the bother of developing anything new.

"We instance metallurgy only by way of illustration. There are plenty of other fields of industry where exactly the same condition exists. We are building the same machines and using the same methods as a dozen years ago, and the real advances in the art are being made by European inventors and manufacturers."

To which President Wilson's statement may be added:

"I am not saying that all invention had been stopped by the growth of trusts, but I think it is perfectly clear that invention in many fields has been discouraged, that inventors have been prevented from reaping the full fruits of their ingenuity and industry, and that mankind has been deprived of many comforts and conveniences, as well as the opportunity of buying at lower prices.

"Do you know, have you had occasion to learn, that there is no hospitality for invention, now-a-days?"

TRUSTS AND FINANCIAL CONCENTRATION

The fact that industrial monopolies arrest development is more serious even than the direct burden imposed through extortionate prices. But the most harm-bearing incident of the trusts is their promotion of financial concentration. Industrial trusts feed the money trust. Practically every trust created has destroyed the financial independence of some communities and of many properties; for it has centered the financing of a large part of whole lines of business in New York, and this usually with one of a few banking houses. This is well illustrated by the Steel Trust, which is a trust of trusts; that is, the Steel Trust combines in one huge holding company the trusts previously formed in the different branches of the steel business. Thus the Tube Trust combined 17 tube mills, located in 16 different cities, scattered over 5 states and owned by 13 different companies. The wire trust combined 19 mills; the sheet steel trust 26; the bridge and structural trust 27; and the tin plate trust 36; all scattered similarly over many states. Finally these and other companies were formed into the United States Steel Corporation, combining 228 companies in all, located in 127 cities and towns, scattered over 18 states. Before the combinations were effected, nearly every one of these companies was owned largely by those who managed it, and had been financed, to a large extent, in the place, or in the state, in which it was located. When the Steel Trust was formed all these concerns came under one management. Thereafter, the financing of each of these 228 corporations (and some which were later acquired) had to be done through or with the consent of J. P. Morgan & Co. *That was the greatest step in financial concentration ever taken.*

STOCK EXCHANGE INCIDENTS

The organization of trusts has served in another way to increase the power of the Money Trust. Few of the independent concerns out of which the trusts have been formed, were listed on the

New York Stock Exchange; and few of them had financial offices in New York. Promoters of large corporations, whose stock is to be held by the public, and also investors, desire to have their securities listed on the New York Stock Exchange. Under the rules of the Exchange, no security can be so listed unless the corporation has a transfer agent and registrar in New York City. Furthermore, banker-directorships have contributed largely to the establishment of the financial offices of the trusts in New York City. That alone would tend to financial concentration. But the listing of the stock enhances the power of the Money Trust in another way. An industrial stock, once listed, frequently becomes the subject of active speculation; and speculation feeds the Money Trust indirectly in many ways. It draws the money of the country to New York. The New York bankers handle the loans of other people's money on the Stock Exchange; and members of the Stock Exchange receive large amounts from commissions. For instance: There are 5,084,952 shares of United States Steel common stock outstanding. But in the five years ending December 31, 1912, speculation in that stock was so extensive that there were sold on the Exchange an average of 29,380,888 shares a year; or nearly six times as much as there is Steel common in existence. Except where the transactions are by or for the brokers, sales on the Exchange involve the payment of twenty-five cents in commission for each share of stock sold; that is, twelve and one-half cents by the seller and twelve and one-half cents by the buyer. Thus the commission from the Steel common alone afforded a revenue averaging many millions a year. The Steel preferred stock is also much traded in; and there are 138 other industrials, largely trusts, listed on the New York Stock Exchange.

TRUST RAMIFICATIONS

But the potency of trusts as a factor in financial concentration is manifested in still other ways; notably through their ramifying operations. This is illustrated forcibly by the General Electric Company's control of water-power companies which has now been disclosed in an able report of the United States Bureau of Corporations:

"The extent of the General Electric influence is not fully revealed by its consolidated balance sheet. A very large number of corporations are connected with it through its subsidiaries and

through corporations controlled by these subsidiaries or affiliated with them.   There is a still
wider circle of influence due to the fact that
officers and directors of the General Electric
Co. and its subsidiaries are also officers or
directors of many other corporations, some of
whose securities are owned by the General
Electric Company.

"The General Electric Company holds in the
first place all the common stock in three security
holding companies: the United Electric Securities
Co., the Electrical Securities Corporation, and
the Electric Bond and Share Co.   Directly and
through these corporations and their officers the
General Electric controls a large part of the
water power of the United States.

. . . "The water-power companies in the
General Electric group are found in 18 States.
These 18 States have 2,325,757 commercial
horsepower developed or under construction,
and of this total the General Electric group includes 939,115 h. p. or 40.4 per cent.   The
greatest amount of power controlled by the
companies in the General Electric group in any
State is found in Washington.   This is followed
by New York, Pennsylvania, California, Montana, Iowa, Oregon, and Colorado.   In five of

the States shown in the table the water-power companies included in the General Electric group control more than 50 per cent. of the commercial power, developed and under construction. The percentage of power in the States included in the General Electric group ranges from a little less than 2 per cent. in Michigan to nearly 80 per cent. in Pennsylvania. In Colorado they control 72 per cent.; in New Hampshire 61 per cent.; in Oregon 58 per cent.; and in Washington 55 per cent.

Besides the power developed and under construction water-power concerns included in the General Electric group own in the States shown in the table 641,600 h. p. undeveloped."

This water power control enables the General Electric group to control other public service corporations:

"The water-power companies subject to General Electric influence control the street railways in at least 16 cities and towns; the electric-light plants in 78 cities and towns; gas plants in 19 cities and towns; and are affiliated with the electric light and gas plants in other towns. Though many of these communities, particularly those served with light only, are

small, several of them are the most important in
the States where these water-power companies
operate. The water-power companies in the
General Electric group own, control, or are
closely affiliated with, the street railways in
Portland and Salem, Ore.; Spokane, Wash.;
Great Falls, Mont.; St. Louis, Mo.; Winona,
Minn.; Milwaukee and Racine, Wis.; Elmira,
N. Y.; Asheville and Raleigh, N. C., and other
relatively less important towns. The towns in
which the lighting plants (electric or gas) are
owned or controlled include Portland, Salem,
Astoria, and other towns in Oregon; Bellingham
and other towns in Washington; Butte, Great
Falls, Bozeman and other towns in Montana;
Leadville and Colorado Springs in Colorado;
St. Louis, Mo.; Milwaukee, Racine and several
small towns in Wisconsin; Hudson and Rens-
selaer, N. Y.; Detroit, Mich.; Asheville and
Raleigh, N. C.; and in fact one or more towns in
practically every community where developed
water power is controlled by this group. In
addition to the public-service corporations thus
controlled by the water-power companies subject
to General Electric influence, there are numerous
public-service corporations in other municipalities
that purchase power from the hydroelectric

developments controlled by or affiliated with the General Electric Co. This is true of Denver, Colo., which has already been discussed. In Baltimore, Md., a water-power concern in the General Electric group, namely, the Pennsylvania Water & Power Co., sells 20,000 h. p. to the Consolidated Gas, Electric Light & Power Co., which controls the entire light and power business of that city. The power to operate all the electric street railway systems of Buffalo, N. Y., and vicinity, involving a trackage of approximately 375 miles, is supplied through a subsidiary of the Niagara Falls Power Co."

And the General Electric Company, through the financing of public service companies, exercises a like influence in communities where there is no water power:

"It, or its subsidiaries, has acquired control of or an interest in the public-service corporations of numerous cities where there is no water-power connection, and it is affiliated with still others by virtue of common directors. . . . This vast network of relationship between hydro-electric corporations through prominent officers and directors of the largest manufacturer of electrical machinery and supplies in the United States is highly significant. . . .

"It is possible that this relationship to such a large number of strong financial concerns, through common officers and directors, affords the General Electric Co. an advantage that may place rivals at a corresponding disadvantage. Whether or not this great financial power has been used to the particular disadvantage of any rival water-power concern is not so important as the fact that such power exists and that it might be so used at any time."

THE SHERMAN LAW

The Money Trust cannot be broken, if we allow its power to be constantly augmented. To break the Money Trust, we must stop that power at its source. The industrial trusts are among its most effective feeders. Those which are illegal should be dissolved. The creation of new ones should be prevented. To this end the Sherman Law should be supplemented both by providing more efficient judicial machinery, and by creating a commission with administrative functions to aid in enforcing the law. When that is done, another step will have been taken toward securing the New Freedom. But restrictive legislation alone will not suffice. We should bear in mind the admonition with which the Commissioner of Corporations closes his review of our water power development:

"There is . . . presented such a situation in water powers and other public utilities as might bring about at any time under a single management the control of a majority of the developed water power in the United States and similar control over the public utilities in a vast number of cities and towns, including some of the most important in the country."

We should conserve all rights which the Federal Government and the States now have in our natural resources, and there should be a complete separation of our industries from railroads and public utilities.

CHAPTER VIII

A CURSE OF BIGNESS

Bigness has been an important factor in the rise of the Money Trust: Big railroad systems, Big industrial trusts, Big public service companies; and as instruments of these Big banks and Big trust companies. J. P. Morgan & Co. (in their letter of defence to the Pujo Committee) urge the needs of Big Business as the justification for financial concentration. They declare that what they euphemistically call "coöperation" is "simply a further result of the necessity for handling great transactions"; that "the country obviously requires not only the larger individual banks, but demands also that those banks shall coöperate to perform efficiently the country's business"; and that "a step backward along this line would mean a halt in industrial progress that would affect every wage-earner from the Atlantic to the Pacific." The phrase "great transactions" is used by the bankers apparently as meaning large corporate security issues.

Leading bankers have undoubtedly coöperated during the last 15 years in floating some very

large security issues, as well as many small ones.
But relatively few large issues were made
necessary by great improvements undertaken or
by industrial development. Improvements and
development ordinarily proceed slowly. For
them, even where the enterprise involves large
expenditures, a series of smaller issues is usually
more appropriate than single large ones. This is
particularly true in the East where the building
of new railroads has practically ceased. The
"great" security issues in which bankers have
coöperated were, with relatively few exceptions,
made either for the purpose of effecting combinations or as a consequence of such combinations. Furthermore, the combinations which
made necessary these large security issues or
underwritings were, in most cases, either contrary
to existing statute law, or contrary to laws recommended by the Interstate Commerce Commission, or contrary to the laws of business efficiency.
So both the financial concentration and the
combinations which they have served were, in
the main, against the public interest. Size,
we are told, is not a crime. But size may, at
least, become noxious by reason of the means
through which it was attained or the uses to
which it is put. And it is size attained by

combination, instead of natural growth, which has contributed so largely to our financial concentration. Let us examine a few cases:

THE HARRIMAN PACIFICS

J. P. Morgan & Co., in urging the "need of large banks and the coöperation of bankers," said:

"The Attorney-General's recent approval of the Union Pacific settlement calls for a single commitment on the part of bankers of $126,000,000."

This $126,000,000 "commitment" was not made to enable the Union Pacific to secure capital. On the contrary it was a guaranty that it would succeed in disposing of its Southern Pacific stock to that amount. And when it had disposed of that stock, it was confronted with the serious problem—what to do with the proceeds? This huge underwriting became necessary solely because the Union Pacific had violated the Sherman Law. It had acquired that amount of Southern Pacific stock illegally; and the Supreme Court of the United States finally decreed that the illegality cease. This same illegal purchase had been the occasion, twelve years earlier, of another "great transaction,"—the issue of a $100,000,000 of Union Pacific bonds, which were sold to provide funds for acquiring this Southern Pacific and other stocks in violation of law. Bankers "coöperated" also to accomplish that.

UNION PACIFIC IMPROVEMENTS

The Union Pacific and its auxiliary lines (the Oregon Short Line, the Oregon Railway and Navigation and the Oregon-Washington Railroad) made, in the fourteen years, ending June 30, 1912, issues of securities aggregating $375,158,183 (of which $46,500,000 were refunded or redeemed); but the large security issues served mainly to supply funds for engaging in illegal combinations or stock speculation. The extraordinary improvements and additions that raised the Union Pacific Railroad to a high state of efficiency were provided mainly by the net earnings from the operation of its railroads. And note how great the improvements and additions were: Tracks were straightened, grades were lowered, bridges were rebuilt, heavy rails were laid, old equipment was replaced by new; and the cost of these was charged largely as operating expense. Additional equipment was added, new lines were built or acquired, increasing the system by 3524 miles of line, and still other improvements and betterments were made and charged to capital

account. These expenditures aggregated $191,-
512,328. But it needed no "large security
issues" to provide the capital thus wisely expended. The net earnings from the operations
of these railroads were so large that nearly all
these improvements and additions could have
been made without issuing on the average more
than $1,000,000 a year of additional securities for
"new money," and the company still could have
paid six per cent. dividends after 1906 (when that
rate was adopted). For while $13,679,452 a
year, on the average, was charged to Cost
of Road and Equipment, the surplus net
earnings and other funds would have yielded, on
the average, $12,750,982 a year available for
improvements and additions, without raising
money on new security issues.

HOW THE SECURITY PROCEEDS WERE SPENT

The $375,000,000 securities (except to the
extent of about $13,000,000 required for im-
provements, and the amounts applied for refunding and redemptions) were available to buy
stocks and bonds of other companies. And some
of the stocks so acquired were sold at large
profits, providing further sums to be employed
in stock purchases.

The $375,000,000 Union Pacific Lines security
issues, therefore, were not needed to supply
funds for Union Pacific improvements; nor did
these issues supply funds for the improvement of
any of the companies in which the Union Pacific
invested (except that certain amounts were
advanced later to aid in financing the Southern
Pacific). *They served, substantially, no purpose
save to transfer the ownership of railroad stocks
from one set of persons to another.*

Here are some of the principal investments:

1. $91,657,500, in acquiring and financing the Southern
   Pacific.
2. $89,391,401, in acquiring the Northern Pacific stock and
   stock of the Northern Securities Co.
3. $45,466,960, in acquiring Baltimore & Ohio stock.
4. $37,692,256, in acquiring Illinois Central stock.
5. $23,205,679, in acquiring New York Central stock.
6. $10,395,000, in acquiring Atchison, Topeka & Santa Fe
   stock.
7. $8,946,781, in acquiring Chicago & Alton stock.
8. $11,610,187, in acquiring Chicago, Milwaukee & St. Paul
   stock.
9. $6,750,423, in acquiring Chicago & Northwestern stock.
10. $6,936,696, in acquiring Railroad Securities Co. stock
    (Illinois Central stock.)

The immediate effect of these stock acquisitions, as stated by the Interstate Commerce
Commission in 1907, was merely this:

"Mr. Harriman may journey by steamship from New York to New Orleans, thence by rail to San Francisco, across the Pacific Ocean to China, and, returning by another route to the United States, may go to Ogden by any one of three rail lines, and thence to Kansas City or Omaha, without leaving the deck or platform of a carrier which he controls, and without duplicating any part of his journey.

"He has further what appears to be a dominant control in the Illinois Central Railroad running directly north from the Gulf of Mexico to the Great Lakes, parallel to the Mississippi River; and two thousand miles west of the Mississippi he controls the only line of railroad parallel to the Pacific Coast, and running from the Colorado River to the Mexican border. . . .

"The testimony taken at this hearing shows that about fifty thousand square miles of territory in the State of Oregon, surrounded by the lines of the Oregon Short Line Railroad Company, the Oregon Railroad and Navigation Company, and the Southern Pacific Company, is not developed. While the funds of those companies which could be used for that purpose are being invested in stocks like the New York Central and other lines having only a remote

relation to the territory in which the Union Pacific
System is located."

Mr. Harriman succeeded in becoming director
in 27 railroads with 39,354 miles of line; and they
extended from the Atlantic to the Pacific; from
the Great Lakes to the Gulf of Mexico.

THE AFTERMATH

On September 9, 1909, less than twelve years
after Mr. Harriman first became a director in the
Union Pacific, he died from overwork at the age
of 61. But it was not death only that had
set a limit to his achievements. The multiplicity
of his interests prevented him from performing
for his other railroads the great services that had
won him a world-wide reputation as manager
and rehabilitator of the Union Pacific and the
Southern Pacific. Within a few months after
Mr. Harriman's death the serious equipment
scandal on the Illinois Central became public,
culminating in the probable suicide of one of the
vice-presidents of that company. The Chicago
& Alton (in the management of which Mr.
Harriman was prominent from 1899 to 1907, as
President, Chairman of the Board, or Executive
Committeeman), has never regained the prosperity it enjoyed before he and his associates

acquired control. The Père Marquette has
passed again into receiver's hands. Long before
Mr. Harriman's death the Union Pacific had
disposed of its Northern Pacific stock, because
the Supreme Court of the United States declared
the Northern Securities Company illegal, and
dissolved the Northern Pacific-Great Northern
merger. Three years after his death, the Supreme Court of the United States ordered the
Union Pacific-Southern Pacific merger dissolved.
By a strange irony, the law has permitted the
Union Pacific to reap large profits from its illegal
transactions in Northern Pacific and Southern
Pacific stocks. But many other stocks held
"as investments" have entailed large losses.
Stocks in the Illinois Central and other companies which cost the Union Pacific $129,894,-
991.72, had on November 15, 1913, a market
value of only $87,851,500; showing a shrinkage
of $42,043,491.72 and the average income from
them, while held, was only about 4.30 per cent.
on their cost.

A BANKERS' PARADISE

Kuhn, Loeb & Co. were the Union Pacific
bankers. It was in pursuance of a promise which
Mr. Jacob H. Schiff—the senior partner—had

given, pending the reorganization, that Mr.
Harriman first became a member of the Executive
Committee in 1897. Thereafter combinations
grew and crumbled, and there were vicissi-
tudes in stock speculations. But the investment
bankers prospered amazingly; and financial concentration proceeded without abatement. The
bankers and their associates received the commissions paid for purchasing the stocks which
the Supreme Court holds to have been acquired
illegally—and have retained them. The bankers
received commissions for underwriting the securities issued to raise the money with which to buy
the stocks which the Supreme Court holds to have
been illegally acquired, and have retained them.
The bankers received commissions paid for floating
securities of the controlled companies—while
they were thus controlled in violation of law—and
have, of course, retained them. Finally when,
after years, a decree is entered to end the illegal
combination, these same bankers are on hand
to perform the services of undertaker—and
receive further commissions for their banker-aid
in enabling the law-breaking corporation to end
its wrong doing and to comply with the decree of
the Supreme Court. And yet, throughout nearly
all this long period, both before and after Mr.

Harriman's death, two partners in Kuhn, Loeb & Co. were directors or members of the executive committee of the Union Pacific; and as such must be deemed responsible with others for the illegal acts.

Indeed, these bankers have not only received commissions for the underwritings of transactions accomplished, though illegal; they have received commissions also for merely *agreeing* to underwrite a "great transaction" which the authorities would not permit to be *accomplished*. The $126,000,000 underwriting (that "single commitment on the part of bankers" to which J. P. Morgan & Co. refer as being called for by "the Attorney General's approval of the Union Pacific settlement") never became effective; because the Public Service Commission of California refused to approve the terms of settlement. But the Union Pacific, nevertheless, paid the Kuhn Loeb Syndicate a large underwriting fee for having been ready and willing "to serve," should the opportunity arise: and another underwriting commission was paid when the Southern Pacific stock was finally distributed, with the approval of Attorney General McReynolds, under the Court's decree. Thus the illegal purchase of Southern Pacific stock yielded directly four crops of commissions; two when it was acquired, and two when it was disposed of. And during the intervening period the illegally controlled Southern Pacific yielded many more commissions to the bankers. For the schedules filed with the Pujo Committee show that Kuhn, Loeb & Co. marketed, in addition to the Union Pacific securities above referred to, $334,000,000 of Southern Pacific and Central Pacific securities between 1903 and 1911.

The aggregate amount of the commissions paid to these bankers in connection with Union Pacific-Southern Pacific transactions is not disclosed. It must have been very large; for not only were the transactions "great"; but the commissions were liberal. The Interstate Commerce Commission finds that bankers received about 5 per cent. on the purchase price for buying the first 750,000 shares of Southern Pacific stock; and the underwriting commission on the first $100,000,000 Union Pacific bonds issued to make that and other purchases was $5,000,000. How large the two underwriting commissions were which the Union Pacific paid in effecting the severance of this illegal merger, both the company and the bankers have declined to disclose. Furthermore the Interstate Commerce Commission showed, clearly, while investigating the Union Pacific's purchase of the Chicago & Alton stock, that the bankers' profits were by no means confined to commissions.

THE BURLINGTON

Such railroad combinations produce injury to the public far more serious than the heavy tax of bankers' commissions and profits. For in nearly every case the absorption into a great system of a theretofore independent railroad has involved the loss of financial independence to some community, property or men, who thereby become subjects or satellites of the Money Trust. The passing of the Chicago, Burlington & Quincy, in 1901, to the Morgan associates, presents a striking example of this process.

After the Union Pacific acquired the Southern Pacific stock in 1901, it sought control, also, of the Chicago, Burlington & Quincy,—a most prosperous railroad, having then 7912 miles of line. The Great Northern and Northern Pacific recognized that Union Pacific control of the Burlington would exclude them from much of Illinois, Missouri, Wisconsin, Kansas, Nebraska, Iowa, and South Dakota. The two northern roads, which were already closely allied with each other and with J. P. Morgan & Co., thereupon purchased for $215,227,000, of their joint 4 per cent. bonds, nearly all of the $109,324,000 (par value) outstanding Burlington stock. A struggle with the Union Pacific ensued which yielded soon to "harmonious coöperation." The Northern Securities Company was formed with $400,000,000 capital, thereby merging the Great Northern, the Northern Pacific and the Burlington, and joining the Harriman, Kuhn-Loeb, with the Morgan-Hill interests. Obviously neither the issue of $215,000,000 joint 4's, nor the issue of the $400,000,000 Northern Securities stock supplied one dollar of funds for improvements of, or additions to, any of the four great railroad systems concerned in these "large transactions." *The sole effect of issuing $615,000,000 of securities was to transfer stock from one set of persons to another.* And the resulting "harmonious cooperation" was soon interrupted by the government proceedings, which ended with the dissolution of the Northern Securities Company. But the evil done outlived the combination. The Burlington had passed forever from its independent Boston owners to the Morgan allies, who remain in control.

The Burlington—one of Boston's finest achievements—was the creation of John M. Forbes. He was a builder; not a combiner, or banker, or wizard of finance. He was a simple, hardworking business man. He had been a merchant in China at a time when China's trade was among America's big business. He had been connected with shipping and with manufactures. He had the imagination of the great merchant; the patience and perseverance of the great manufacturer; the courage of the sea-farer; and the broad view of the statesman. Bold, but never reckless; scrupulously careful of other people's money, he was ready, after due weighing of chances, to risk his own in enterprises promising success. He was in the best sense of the term, a great adventurer. Thus equipped, Mr. Forbes entered, in 1852, upon those railroad enterprises which later developed into the Chicago, Burlington & Quincy. Largely with his own money and that of friends who confided in him, he built these railroads and carried them through the panic of '57, when the "great banking houses" of those days lacked courage to assume the burdens of a struggling ill-constructed line, staggering under financial difficulties.

Under his wise management, and that of the men whom he trained, the little Burlington became a great system. It was "built on honor," and managed honorably. It weathered every other great financial crisis, as it did that of 1857. It reached maturity without a reorganization or the sacrifice of a single stockholder or bondholder.

Investment bankers had no place on the Burlington Board of Directors; nor had the banker-practice, of being on both sides of a bargain. "I am unwilling," said Mr. Forbes, early in his career, "to run the risk of having the imputation of buying from a company in which I am interested." About twenty years later he made his greatest fight to rescue the Burlington from the control of certain contractor-directors, whom his biographer, Mr. Pearson, describes as "persons of integrity, who had conceived that in their twofold capacity as contractors and directors they were fully able to deal with themselves justly." Mr. Forbes thought otherwise. The stockholders, whom he had aroused, sided with him and he won.

Mr. Forbes was the pioneer among Boston railroad-builders. His example and his success inspired many others, for Boston was not lacking

then in men who were builders, though some
lacked his wisdom, and some his character.   Her
enterprise and capital constructed, in large part,
the Union Pacific, the Atchison, the Mexican
Central, the Wisconsin Central, and 24 other
railroads in the West and South.   One by one
these western and southern railroads passed out
of Boston control; the greater part of them into
the control of the Morgan allies.   Before the
Burlington was surrendered, Boston had begun
to lose her dominion, even, over the railroads of
New England.   In 1900 the Boston & Albany
was leased to the New York Central,—a Morgan
property; and a few years later, another Morgan
railroad—the New Haven—acquired control of
nearly every other transportation line in New
England.   Now nothing is left of Boston's
railroad dominion in the West and South,
except the Eastern Kentucky Railroad—a line
36 miles long; and her control of the railroads of
Massachusetts is limited to the Grafton & Upton
with 19 miles of line and the Boston, Revere
Beach & Lynn,—a passenger road 13 miles long.

THE NEW HAVEN MONOPOLY

The rise of the New Haven Monopoly presents
another striking example of combination as a

developer of financial concentration; and it illustrates also the use to which "large security issues" are put.

In 1892, when Mr. Morgan entered the New Haven directorate, it was a very prosperous little railroad with capital liabilities of $25,000,000 paying 10 per cent. dividends, and operating 508 miles of line. By 1899 the capitalization had grown to $80,477,600, but the aggregate mileage had also grown (mainly through merger or leases of other lines) to 2017. Fourteen years later, in 1913, when Mr. Morgan died and Mr. Mellen resigned, the mileage was 1997, just 20 miles less than in 1899; but the capital liabilities had increased to $425,935,000. Of course the business of the railroad had grown largely in those fourteen years; the road-bed was improved, bridges built, additional tracks added, and much equipment purchased; and for all this, new capital was needed; and additional issues were needed, also, because the company paid out in dividends more than it earned. But of the capital increase, over $200,000,000 was expended in the acquisition of the stock or other securities of some 121 other railroads, steamships, street railway-, electric-light-, gas- and water-companies. It was these outside properties, which made necessary the much discussed $67,000,000, 6 per cent. bond issue, as well as other large and expensive security issues. For in these fourteen years the improvements on the railroad including new equipment have cost, on the average, only $10,000,000 a year.

THE NEW HAVEN BANKERS

Few, if any, of those 121 companies which the New Haven acquired had, prior to their absorption by it, been financed by J. P. Morgan & Co. The needs of the Boston & Maine and Maine Central—the largest group—had, for generations, been met mainly through their own stockholders or through Boston banking houses. No investment banker had been a member of the Board of Directors of either of those companies. The New York, Ontario & Western—the next largest of the acquired railroads—had been financed in New York, but by persons apparently entirely independent of the Morgan allies. The smaller Connecticut railroads, now combined in the Central New England, had been financed mainly in Connecticut, or by independent New York bankers. The financing of the street railway companies had been done largely by individual financiers, or

by small and independent bankers in the states
or cities where the companies operate. Some of
the steamship companies had been financed by
their owners, some through independent bankers.
As the result of the absorption of these 121 companies into the New Haven system, the financing
of all these railroads, steamship companies,
street railways, and other corporations, was
made tributary to J. P. Morgan & Co.; and the
independent bankers were eliminated or became
satellites. *And this financial concentration was
proceeded with, although practically every one
of these 121 companies was acquired by the New
Haven in violation either of the state or federal
law, or of both.* Enforcement of the Sherman
Act will doubtless result in dissolving this
unwieldy illegal combination.

THE COAL MONOPOLY

Proof of the "coöperation" of the anthracite
railroads is furnished by the ubiquitous presence
of George F. Baker on the Board of Directors
of the Reading, the Jersey Central, the Lackawanna, the Lehigh, the Erie, and the New York,
Susquehanna & Western railroads, which together control nearly all the unmined anthracite
as well as the actual tonnage. These roads have

been an important factor in the development of the Money Trust.   They are charged by the Department of Justice with fundamental violations both of the Sherman Law and of the Commodity clause of the Hepburn Act, which prohibits a railroad from carrying, in interstate trade, any commodity in which it has an interest, direct or indirect.   Nearly every large issue of securities made in the last 14 years by any of these railroads (except the Erie), has been in connection with some act of combination.   The combination of the anthracite railroads to suppress the construction, through the Temple Iron Company, of a competing coal road, has already been declared illegal by the Supreme Court of the United States.   And in the bituminous coal field—the Kanawha District—the United States Circuit Court of Appeals has recently decreed that a similar combination by the Lake Shore, the Chesapeake & Ohio, and the Hocking Valley, be dissolved.

OTHER RAILROAD COMBINATIONS

The cases of the Union Pacific and of the New Haven are typical—not exceptional.   Our railroad history presents numerous instances of large security issues made wholly or mainly to effect combinations. Some of these combinations have been proper as a means of securing natural feeders or extensions of main lines. But far more of them have been dictated by the desire to suppress active or potential competition; or by personal ambition or greed; or by the mistaken belief that efficiency grows with size.

Thus the monstrous combination of the Rock Island and the St. Louis and San Francisco with over 14,000 miles of line is recognized now to have been obviously inefficient. It was severed voluntarily; but, had it not been, must have crumbled soon from inherent defects, if not as a result of proceedings under the Sherman law. Both systems are suffering now from the effects of this unwise combination; the Frisco, itself greatly overcombined, has paid the penalty in receivership. The Rock Island—a name once expressive of railroad efficiency and stability—has, through its excessive recapitalizations and combinations, become a football of speculators, and a source of great apprehension to confiding investors. The combination of the Cincinnati, Hamilton and Dayton, and the Père Marquette led to several receiverships.

There are, of course, other combinations which have not been disastrous to the owners of the railroads. But the fact that a railroad combination has not been disastrous does not necessarily justify it. The evil of the concentration of power is obvious; and as combination necessarily involves such concentration of power, the burden of justifying a combination should be placed upon those who seek to effect it.

For instance, what public good has been subserved by allowing the Atlantic Coast Line Railroad Company to issue $50,000,000 of securities to acquire control of the Louisville & Nashville Railroad—a widely extended, self-sufficient system of 5000 miles, which, under the wise management of President Milton H. Smith had prospered continuously for many years before the acquisition; and which has gross earnings nearly twice as large as those of the Atlantic Coast Line. The legality of this combination has been recently challenged by Senator Lea; and an investigation by the Interstate Commerce Commission has been ordered.

THE PENNSYLVANIA

The reports from the Pennsylvania suggest the inquiry whether even this generally well-managed railroad is not suffering from excessive bigness. After 1898 it, too, bought, in large amounts, stocks in other railroads, including the Chesapeake & Ohio, the Baltimore & Ohio, and the Norfolk & Western. In 1906 it sold all its Chesapeake & Ohio stock, and a majority of its Baltimore & Ohio and Norfolk & Western holdings. Later it reversed its policy and resumed stock purchases, acquiring, among others, more Norfolk & Western and New York, New Haven & Hartford; and on Dec. 31, 1912, held securities valued at $331,909,154.32; of which, however, a large part represents Pennsylvania System securities. These securities (mostly stocks) constitute about one-third of the total assets of the Pennsylvania Railroad. The income on these securities in 1912 averaged only 4.30 per cent. on their valuation, while the Pennsylvania paid 6 per cent. on its stock. But the cost of carrying these foreign stocks is not limited to the difference between this income and outgo. To raise money on these stocks the Pennsylvania had to issue its own securities; and there is such a thing as an over-supply even of Pennsylvania securities. Over-supply of any stock depresses market values, and increases the cost to the Pennsylvania of raising new money. Recently came the welcome announcement of the management that it will dispose of its stocks in the anthracite coal mines; and it is intimated that it will divest itself also of other holdings in companies (like the Cambria Steel Company) extraneous to the business of railroading. This policy should be extended to include the disposition also of all stock in other railroads (like the Norfolk & Western, the Southern Pacific and the New Haven) which are not a part of the Pennsylvania System.

RECOMMENDATIONS

Six years ago the Interstate Commerce Commission, after investigating the Union Pacific transaction above referred to, recommended legislation to remedy the evils there disclosed. Upon concluding recently its investigation of the New Haven, the Commission repeated and amplified those recommendations, saying:

"No student of the railroad problem can doubt that a most prolific source of financial disaster and complication to railroads in the past has been the desire and ability of railroad managers to engage in enterprises outside the legitimate operation of their railroads, especially by the acquisition of other railroads and their securities. The evil which results, first, to the investing public, and, finally, to the general public, cannot be corrected after the transaction has taken place; it can be easily and effectively prohibited. In our opinion the following propositions lie at the foundation of all adequate regulation of interstate railroads:

1. Every interstate railroad should be prohibited from spending money or incurring liability or acquiring property not in the operation of its railroad or in the legitimate improvement, extension, or development of that railroad.

2. No interstate railroad should be permitted to lease or purchase any other railroad, nor to acquire the stocks or securities of any other railroad, nor to guarantee the same, directl or indirectly, without the approval of the federal government.

3. No stocks or bonds should be issued by an interstate railroad except for the purposes sanctioned in the two preceding paragraphs, and none should be issued without the approval of the federal government.

It may be unwise to attempt to specify the price at which and the manner in which railroad stocks and securities shall be disposed of; but it is easy and safe to define the purpose for which they may be issued and to confine the expenditure of the money realized to that purpose."

These recommendations are in substantial accord with those adopted by the National

Association of Railway Commissioners. They should be enacted into law. And they should be supplemented by amendments of the Commodity Clause of the Hepburn Act, so that:

1. Railroads will be effectually prohibited from owning stock in corporations whose products they transport;

2. Such corporations will be prohibited from owning important stockholdings in railroads; and

3. Holding companies will be prohibited from controlling, as does the Reading, both a railroad and corporations whose commodities it transports.

If laws such as these are enacted and duly enforced, we shall be protected from a recurrence of tragedies like the New Haven, of domestic scandals like the Chicago and Alton, and of international ones like the Frisco. We shall also escape from that inefficiency which is attendant upon excessive size. But what is far more important, we shall, by such legislation, remove a potent factor in financial concentration. Decentralization will begin. The liberated smaller units will find no difficulty in financing their needs without bowing the knee to money lords. And a long step will have been taken toward attainment of the New Freedom.

CHAPTER IX

THE FAILURE OF BANKER-MANAGEMENT

THERE is not one moral, but many, to be drawn from the Decline of the New Haven and the Fall of Mellen. That history offers texts for many sermons. It illustrates the Evils of Monopoly, the Curse of Bigness, the Futility of Lying, and the Pitfalls of Law-Breaking. But perhaps the most impressive lesson that it should teach to investors is the failure of banker-management.

BANKER CONTROL

For years J. P. Morgan & Co. were the fiscal agents of the New Haven. For years Mr. Morgan was *the* director of the Company. He gave to that property probably closer personal attention than to any other of his many interests. Stockholders' meetings are rarely interesting or important; and few indeed must have been the occasions when Mr. Morgan attended any stockholders' meeting of other companies in which he was a director. But it was his habit, when in

America, to be present at meetings of the New
Haven.   In 1907, when the policy of monopolistic
expansion was first challenged, and again at the
meeting in 1909 (after Massachusetts had un-
wisely accorded its sanction to the Boston &
Maine merger), Mr. Morgan himself moved
the large increases of stock which were unani-
mously voted. Of course, he attended the
important directors' meetings.   His will was
law. President Mellen indicated this in his
statement before Interstate Commerce Commissioner Prouty, while discussing the New
York, Westchester & Boston—the railroad without a terminal in New York, which cost the
New Haven $1,500,000 a mile to acquire, and
was then costing it, in operating deficits and
interest charges, $100,000 a month to run:

"I am in a very embarrassing position, Mr.
Commissioner, regarding the New York, Westchester & Boston. I have never been enthusiastic or at all optimistic of its being a good investment for our company in the present, or in the
immediate future; but people in whom I had
greater confidence than I have in myself thought
it was wise and desirable; I yielded my judgment;
indeed, I don't know that it would have made
much difference whether I yielded or not."

THE BANKERS' RESPONSIBILITY

Bankers are credited with being a conservative force in the community. The tradition lingers that they are preëminently "safe and sane." And yet, the most grievous fault of this banker-managed railroad has been its financial recklessness—a fault that has already brought heavy losses to many thousands of small investors throughout New England for whom bankers are supposed to be natural guardians. In a community where its railroad stocks have for generations been deemed absolutely safe investments, the passing of the New Haven and of the Boston & Maine dividends after an unbroken dividend record of generations comes as a disaster.

This disaster is due mainly to enterprises outside the legitimate operation of these railroads; for no railroad company has equaled the New Haven in the quantity and extravagance of its outside enterprises. But it must be remembered, that neither the president of the New Haven nor any other railroad manager could engage in such transactions without the sanction of the Board of Directors. It is the directors, not Mr. Mellen, who should bear the responsibility.

Close scrutiny of the transactions discloses no justification. On the contrary, scrutiny serves only to make more clear the gravity of the errors committed. Not merely were recklessly extravagant acquisitions made in mad pursuit of monopoly; but the financial judgment, the financiering itself, was conspicuously bad. To pay for property several times what it is worth, to engage in grossly unwise enterprises, are errors of which no conservative directors should be found guilty; for perhaps the most important function of directors is to test the conclusions and curb by calm counsel the excessive zeal of too ambitious managers. But while we have no right to expect from bankers exceptionally good judgment in ordinary business matters; we do have a right to expect from them prudence, reasonably good financiering, and insistence upon straightforward accounting. And it is just the lack of these qualities in the New Haven management to which the severe criticism of the Interstate Commerce Commission is particularly directed.

Conmissioner Prouty calls attention to the vast increase of capitalization. During the nine years beginning July 1, 1903, the capital of the New York, New Haven & Hartford Railroad

Company itself increased from $93,000,000 to
about $417,000,000 (excluding premiums). That
fact alone would not convict the management
of reckless financiering; but the fact that so
little of the new capital was represented by stock
might well raise a question as to its conservative-
ness. For the indebtedness (including guaran-
ties) was increased over twenty times (from
about $14,000,000 to $300,000,000), while the
stock outstanding in the hands of the public
was not doubled ($80,000,000 to $158,000,000).
Still, in these days of large things, even such
growth of corporate liabilities might be consistent with "safe and sane management."

But what can be said in defense of the financial judgment of the banker-management under
which these two railroads find themselves con-
fronted, in the fateful year 1913, with a most
disquieting floating indebtedness? On March
31, the New Haven had outstanding $43,000,000
in short-time notes; the Boston & Maine had
then outstanding $24,500,000, which have been
increased since to $27,000,000; and additional
notes have been issued by several of its subsidiary lines. Mainly to meet its share of these
loans, the New Haven, which before its great
expansion could sell at par 3 1/2 per cent. bonds

convertible into stock at $150 a share, was so
eager to issue at par $67,500,000 of its 6 per
cent. 20-year bonds convertible into stock as to
agree to pay J. P. Morgan & Co. a 2 1/2 per
cent. underwriting commission. True, money
was "tight" then. But is it not very bad
financiering to be so unprepared for the "tight"
money market which had been long expected?
Indeed, the New Haven's management, particularly, ought to have avoided such an error; for
it committed a similar one in the "tight" money
market of 1907–1908, when it had to sell at par
$39,000,000 of its 6 per cent. 40-year bonds.

These huge short-time borrowings of the System were not due to unexpected emergencies or
to their monetary conditions. They were of
gradual growth. On June 30, 1910, the two
companies owed in short-term notes only $10,-
180,364; by June 30, 1911, the amount had grown
to $30,759,959; by June 30, 1912, to $45,395,000;
and in 1913 to over $70,000,000. Of course the
rate of interest on the loans increased also
very largely. And these loans were incurred
unnecessarily. They represent, in the main,
not improvements on the New Haven or on the
Boston & Maine Railroads, but money borrowed
either to pay for stocks in other companies which

these companies could not afford to buy, or to pay dividends which had not been earned.

In five years out of the last six the New Haven Railroad has, on its own showing, paid dividends in excess of the year's earnings; and the annual deficits disclosed would have been much larger if proper charges for depreciation of equipment and of steamships had been made.   In each of the last three years, during which the New Haven had absolute control of the Boston & Maine, the latter paid out in dividends so much in excess of earnings that before April, 1913, the surplus accumulated in earlier years had been converted into a deficit.

Surely these facts show, at least, an extra-ordinary lack of financial prudence.

WHY BANKER-MANAGEMENT FAILED

Now, how can the failure of the banker-management of the New Haven be explained?

A few have questioned the ability; a few the integrity of the bankers.   Commissioner Prouty attributed the mistakes made to the Company's pursuit of a transportation monopoly.

"The reason," says he, "is as apparent as the fact itself.   The present management of that Company started out with the purpose of controlling the transportation facilities of New England. In the accomplishment of that purpose it bought what must be had and paid what must be paid. To this purpose and its attempted execution can be traced every one of these financial misfortunes and derelictions."

But it still remains to find the cause of the bad judgment exercised by the eminent banker-management in entering upon and in carrying out the policy of monopoly. For there were as grave errors in the execution of the policy of monopoly as in its adoption. Indeed, it was the aggregation of important errors of detail which compelled first the reduction, then the passing of dividends and which ultimately impaired the Company's credit.

The failure of the banker-management of the New Haven cannot be explained as the short-comings of individuals. The failure was not accidental. It was not exceptional. It was the natural result of confusing the functions of banker and business man.

UNDIVIDED LOYALTY

The banker should be detached from the business for which he performs the banking service. This detachment is desirable, in the first place, in order to avoid conflict of interest. The relation of banker-directors to corporations which they finance has been a subject of just criticism. Their conflicting interests necessarily prevent single-minded devotion to the corporation. When a banker-director of a railroad decides as railroad man that it shall issue securities, and then sells them to himself as banker, fixing the price at which they are to be taken, there is necessarily grave danger that the interests of the railroad may suffer—suffer both through issuing of securities which ought not to be issued, and from selling them at a price less favorable to the company than should have been obtained. For it is ordinarily impossible for a banker-director to judge impartially between the corporation and himself. Even if he succeeded in being impartial, the relation would not conduce to the best interests of the company. The best bargains are made when buyer and seller are represented by different persons.

DETACHMENT AN ESSENTIAL

But the objection to banker-management does not rest wholly, or perhaps mainly, upon the importance of avoiding divided loyalty. A complete detachment of the banker from the corpo-

ration is necessary in order to secure for the
railroad the benefit of the clearest financial
judgment; for the banker's judgment will be
necessarily clouded by participation in the
management or by ultimate responsibility for
the policy actually pursued. It is *outside* financial advice which the railroad needs.

Long ago it was recognized that "a man who
is his own lawyer has a fool for a client." The
essential reason for this is that soundness of
judgment is easily obscured by self-interest.
Similarly, it is not the proper function of the
banker to construct, purchase, or operate railroads, or to engage in industrial enterprises.
The proper function of the banker is to give to
or to withhold credit from other concerns; to
purchase or to refuse to purchase securities from
other concerns; and to sell securities to other
customers. The proper exercise of this function
demands that the banker should be wholly detached from the concern whose credit or securities are under consideration. His decision to
grant or to withhold credit, to purchase or not
to purchase securities, involves passing judgment on the efficiency of the management or the
soundness of the enterprise; and he ought not
to occupy a position where in so doing he is

passing judgment on himself. Of course detachment does not imply lack of knowledge. The banker should act only with full knowledge, just as a lawyer should act only with full knowledge. The banker who undertakes to make loans to or purchase securities from a railroad for sale to his other customers ought to have as full knowledge of its affairs as does its legal adviser. But the banker should not be, in any sense, his own client. He should not, in the capacity of banker, pass judgment upon the wisdom of his own plans or acts as railroad man.

Such a detached attitude on the part of the banker is demanded also in the interest of his other customers—the purchasers of corporate securities. The investment banker stands toward a large part of his customers in a position of trust, which should be fully recognized. The small investors, particularly the women, who are holding an ever-increasing proportion of our corporate securities, commonly buy on the recommendation of their bankers. The small investors do not, and in most cases cannot, ascertain for themselves the facts on which to base a proper judgment as to the soundness of securities offered. And even if these investors were furnished with the facts, they lack the business

experience essential to forming a proper judgment. Such investors need and are entitled to
have the bankers' advice, and obviously their
unbiased advice; and the advice cannot be unbiased where the banker, as part of the corporation's management, has participated in the creation of the securities which are the subject of
sale to the investor.

Is it conceivable that the great house of Morgan would have aided in providing the New
Haven with the hundreds of millions so un-
wisely expended, if its judgment had not been
clouded by participation in the New Haven's
management?

CHAPTER X

THE INEFFICIENCY OF THE OLIGARCHS

We must break the Money Trust or the Money Trust will break us.

THE Interstate Commerce Commission said in its report on the most disastrous of the recent wrecks on the New Haven Railroad:

"On this directorate were and are men whom the confiding public recognize as magicians in the art of finance, and wizards in the construction, operation, and consolidation of great systems of railroads. The public therefore rested secure that with the knowledge of the railroad art possessed by such men investments and travel should both be safe. Experience has shown that this reliance of the public was not justified as to either finance or safety."

This failure of banker-management is not surprising. The surprise is that men should have supposed it would succeed. For banker-management contravenes the fundamental laws of human limitations: *First*, that no man can serve two masters; *second*, that a man cannot at the same time do many things well.

SEEMING SUCCESSES

There are numerous seeming exceptions to these rules; and a relatively few real ones. Of course, many banker-managed properties have been prosperous; some for a long time, at the expense of the public; some for a shorter time, because of the impetus attained before they were banker-managed. It is not difficult to have a large net income, where one has the field to oneself, has all the advantages privilege can give, and may "charge all the traffic will bear." And even in competitive business the success of a long-established, well-organized business with a widely extended good-will, must continue for a considerable time; especially if buttressed by intertwined relations constantly giving it the preference over competitors. The real test of efficiency comes when success has to be struggled for; when natural or legal conditions limit the charges which may be made for the goods sold or service rendered. Our banker-managed railroads have recently been subjected to such a test, and they have failed to pass it.

"It is only," says Goethe, "when working within limitations, that the master is disclosed."

Banker-management fails, partly because the private interest destroys soundness of judgment and undermines loyalty. It fails partly, also, because banker directors are led by their occupation (and often even by the mere fact of their location remote from the operated properties) to apply a false test in making their decisions. Prominent in the banker-director mind is always this thought: "What will be the probable effect of our action upon the market value of the company's stock and bonds, or, indeed, generally upon stock exchange values?" The stock market is so much a part of the investment-banker's life, that he cannot help being affected by this consideration, however disinterested he may be. The stock market is sensitive. Facts are often misinterpreted "by the street" or by investors. And with the best of intentions, directors susceptible to such influences are led to unwise decisions in the effort to prevent misinterpretations. Thus, expenditures necessary for maintenance, or for the ultimate good of a property are often deferred by banker-directors, because of the belief that the making of them *now*, would (by showing smaller net earnings), create a bad, and even false, impression on the market. Dividends are paid which should not be, because of the effect which it is believed reduction or suspension would have upon the market value of the company's securities. To excerise a sound judgment in the difficult affairs of business is, at best, a delicate operation. And no man can successfully perform that function whose mind is diverted, however innocently, from the study of, "what is best in the long run for the company of which I am director?" The banker-director is peculiarly liable to such distortion of judgment by reason of his occupation and his environment. But there is a further reason why, ordinarily, banker-management must fail.

THE ELEMENT OF TIME

The banker, with his multiplicity of interests, cannot ordinarily give the time essential to proper supervision and to acquiring that knowledge of the facts necessary to the exercise of sound judgment. The *Century Dictionary* tells us that a Director is "one who directs; one who guides, superintends, governs and manages." Real efficiency in any business in which conditions are ever changing must ultimately depend, in large measure, upon the correctness of the judgment exercised, almost from day to day, on the important problems as they arise. And how can the leading bankers, necessarily engrossed in the problems of their own vast private businesses, get time to know and to correlate the facts concerning so many other complex businesses? Besides, they start usually with ignorance of the particular business which they are supposed to direct. When the last paper was signed which created the Steel Trust, one of the lawyers (as Mr. Perkins frankly tells us) said: "That signature is the last one necessary to put the Steel industry, on a large scale, into the hands of men who do not know anything about it."

AVOCATIONS OF THE OLIGARCHS

The New Haven System is not a railroad, but an agglomeration of a railroad plus 121 separate corporations, control of which was acquired by the New Haven after that railroad attained its full growth of about 2000 miles of line. In administering the railroad and each of the properties formerly managed through these 122 separate companies, there must arise from time to time difficult questions on which the directors should pass judgment. The real managing directors of the New Haven system during the decade of its decline were: J. Pierpont Morgan, George F. Baker, and William Rockefeller. Mr. Morgan was, until his death in 1913, the head of perhaps the largest banking house in the world. Mr. Baker was, until 1909, President and then Chairman of the Board of Directors of one of America's leading banks (the First National of New York), and Mr. Rockefeller was, until 1911, President of the Standard Oil Company. Each was well advanced in years. Yet each of these men, besides the duties of his own vast business, and important private interests, undertook to "guide, superintend, govern and manage," not only the New Haven but also the following other corporations, some of which were similarly complex: Mr. Morgan, 48 corporations, including 40 railroad corporations, with at least 100 subsidiary companies, and 16,000 miles of line; 3 banks and trust or insurance companies; 5 industrial and public-service companies. Mr. Baker, 48 corporations, including 15 railroad corporations, with at least 158 subsidiaries, and 37,400 miles of track; 18 banks, and trust or insurance companies; 15 public-service corporations and industrial concerns. Mr. Rockefeller, 37 corporations, including 23 railroad corporations with at least 117 subsidiary companies, and 26,400 miles of line; 5 banks, trust or insurance companies; 9 public service companies and industrial concerns.

SUBSTITUTES

It has been urged that in view of the heavy burdens which the leaders of finance assume in directing Business-America, we should be patient of error and refrain from criticism, lest the leaders be deterred from continuing to perform this public service. A very respectable Boston daily said a few days after Commissioner McChord's report on the North Haven wreck:

"It is believed that the New Haven pillory repeated with some frequency will make the part of railroad director quite undesirable and hard to fill, and more and more avoided by responsible men. Indeed it may even become so that men will have to be paid a substantial salary to compensate them in some degree for the risk involved in being on the board of directors."

But there is no occasion for alarm. The American people have as little need of oligarchy

in business as in politics. There are thousands
of men in America who could have performed
for the New Haven stockholders the task of
one "who guides, superintends, governs and
manages," better than did Mr. Morgan. Mr.
Baker and Mr. Rockefeller. For though possessing less native ability, even the average
business man would have done better than they,
because working under proper conditions. There
is great strength in serving with singleness of
purpose one master only. There is great strength
in having time to give to a business the attention which its difficult problems demand. And
tens of thousands more Americans could be rendered competent to guide our important businesses. Liberty is the greatest developer. Herod-
otus tells us that while the tyrants ruled, the
Athenians were no better fighters than their
neighbors; but when freed, they immediately
surpassed all others. If industrial democracy—
true coöperation—should be substituted for industrial absolutism, there would be no lack of
industrial leaders.

ENGLAND'S BIG BUSINESS

England, too, has big business. But her big
business is the Coöperative Wholesale Society,

with a wonderful story of 50 years of beneficent
growth. Its annual turnover is now about
$150,000,000—an amount exceeded by the sales
of only a few American industrials; an amount
larger than the gross receipts of any American railroad, except the Pennsylvania and
the New York Central systems. Its business
is very diversified, for its purpose is to supply
the needs of its members. It includes that of
wholesale dealer, of manufacturer, of grower,
of miner, of banker, of insurer and of carrier.
It operates the biggest flour mills and the biggest
shoe factory in all Great Britain. It manufactures woolen cloths, all kinds of men's, women's
and children's clothing, a dozen kinds of pre-
pared foods, and as many household articles.
It operates creameries. It carries on every
branch of the printing business. It is now
buying coal lands. It has a bacon factory in
Denmark, and a tallow and oil factory in Australia. It grows tea in Ceylon. And through
all the purchasing done by the Society runs this
general principle: Go direct to the source of
production, whether at home or abroad, so as
to save commissions of middlemen and agents.
Accordingly, it has buyers and warehouses in
the United States, Canada, Australia, Spain, Den-

mark and Sweden. It owns steamers plying
between Continental and English ports. It has
an important banking department; it insures the
property and person of its members. Every
one of these departments is conducted in competition with the most efficient concerns in their
respective lines in Great Britain. The Coöperative Wholesale Society makes its purchases, and
manufactures its products, in order to supply
the 1399 local distributive, coöperative societies
scattered over all England; but each local society
is at liberty to buy from the wholesale society,
or not, as it chooses; and they buy only if
the Coöperative Wholesale sells at market prices.
This the Coöperative actually does; and it is
able besides to return to the local a fair dividend
on its purchases.

INDUSTRIAL DEMOCRACY

Now, how are the directors of this great business chosen?   Not by England's leading bankers,
or other notabilities, supposed to possess unusual
wisdom; but democratically, by all of the people
interested in the operations of the Society.   And
the number of such persons who have directly or
indirectly a voice in the selection of the directors
of the English Coöperative Wholesale Society is

2,750,000. For the directors of the Wholesale Society are elected by vote of the delegates of the 1399 retail societies. And the delegates of the retail societies are, in turn, selected by the members of the local societies;—that is, by the consumers, on the principle of one man, one vote, regardless of the amount of capital contributed. Note what kind of men these industrial democrats select to exercise executive control of their vast organization. Not all-wise bankers or their dummies, but men who have risen from the ranks of coöperation; men who, by conspicuous service in the local societies have won the respect and confidence of their fellows. The directors are elected for one year only; but a director is rarely unseated. J. T. W. Mitchell was president of the Society continuously for 21 years. Thirty-two directors are selected in this manner. Each gives to the business of the Society his whole time and attention; and the aggregate salaries of the thirty-two is less than that of many a single executive in American corporations; for these directors of England's big business serve each for a salary of about $1500 a year.

The Coöperative Wholesale Society of England is the oldest and largest of these institutions. But similar wholesale societies exist in 15 other countries. The Scotch Society (which William Maxwell has served most efficiently as President for thirty years at a salary never exceeding $38 a week) has a turn-over of more than $50,000,000 a year.

A REMEDY FOR TRUSTS

Albert Sonnichsen, General Secretary of the Coöperative League, tells in the *American Review of Reviews* for April, 1913, how the Swedish Wholesale Society curbed the Sugar Trust; how it crushed the Margerine Combine (compelling it to dissolve after having lost 2,300,000 crowns in the struggle); and how in Switzerland the Wholesale Society forced the dissolution of the Shoe Manufacturers Association. He tells also this memorable incident:

"Six years ago, at an international congress in Cremona, Dr. Hans Müller, a Swiss delegate, presented a resolution by which an international wholesale society should be created. Luigi Luzzatti, Italian Minister of State and an ardent member of the movement, was in the chair. Those who were present say Luzzatti paused, his eyes lighted up, then, dramatically raising his hand, he said: 'Dr. Müller proposes to the assem-

bly a great idea—that of opposing to the great
trusts, the Rockefellers of the world, a world-
wide coöperative alliance which shall become so
powerful as to crush the trusts.'"

COÖPERATION IN AMERICA

America has no Wholesale Coöperative Society
able to grapple with the trusts.   But it has some
very strong retail societies, like the Tamarack
of Michigan, which has distributed in dividends
to its members $1,144,000 in 23 years.   The
recent high cost of living has greatly stimulated
interest in the coöperative movement; and John
Graham Brooks reports that we have already
about 350 local distributive societies.   The movement toward federation is progressing.   There
are over 100 coöperative stores in Minnesota,
Wisconsin and other Northwestern states, many
of which were organized by or through the zealous
work of Mr. Tousley and his associates of the
Right Relationship League and are in some ways
affiliated.   In New York City 83 organizations
are affiliated with the Coöperative League.   In
New Jersey the societies have federated into the
American Coöperative Alliance of Northern New
Jersey.   In California, long the seat of effective
cooperative work, a central management com-

mittee is developing.   And progressive Wisconsin
has recently legislated wisely to develop coöperation throughout the state.

Among our farmers the interest in coöperation
is especially keen.   The federal government has
just established a separate bureau of the Department of Agriculture to aid in the study, development and introduction of the best methods
of coöperation in the working of farms, in buying,
and in distribution; and special attention is now
being given to farm credits—a field of coöperation in which Continental Europe has achieved
complete success, and to which David Lubin,
America's delegate to the International Institute
of Agriculture at Rome, has, among others, done
much to direct our attention.

PEOPLE'S SAVINGS BANKS

The German farmer has achieved democratic
banking.   The 13,000 little coöperative credit
associations, with an average membership of
about 90 persons, are truly banks of the people,
by the people and for the people.

First: The banks' resources are *of* the people.
These aggregate about $500,000,000.   Of this
amount $375,000,000 represents the farmers'
savings deposits; $50,000,000, the farmers' cur-

rent deposits; $6,000,000, the farmers' share capital; and $13,000,000, amounts earned and placed in the reserve. Thus, nearly nine-tenths of these large resources belong to the farmers—that is, to the members of the banks.

Second: The banks are managed *by* the people —that is, the members. And membership is easily attained; for the average amount of paid-up share capital was, in 1909, less than $5 per member. Each member has one vote regardless of the number of his shares or the amount of his deposits. These members elect the officers. The committees and trustees (and often even, the treasurer) serve without pay: so that the expenses of the banks are, on the average, about $150 a year.

Third: The banks are *for* the people. The farmers' money is loaned by the farmer to the farmer at a low rate of interest (usually 4 per cent. to 6 per cent.); the shareholders receiving, on their shares, the same rate of interest that the borrowers pay on their loans. Thus the resources of all farmers are made available to each farmer, for productive purposes.

This democratic rural banking is not confined to Germany. As Henry W. Wolff says in his book on coöperative banks:

"Propagating themselves by their own merits, little people's coöperative banks have overspread Germany, Italy, Austria, Hungary, Switzerland, Belgium.   Russia is following up those countries; France is striving strenuously for the possession of coöperative credit.   Servia, Roumania, and Bulgaria have made such credit their own. Canada has scored its first success on the road to its acquisition.   Cyprus, and even Jamaica, have made their first start.   Ireland has substantial first-fruits to show of her economic sowings.

"South Africa is groping its way to the same goal.   Egypt has discovered the necessity of coöperative banks, even by the side of Lord Cromer's pet creation, the richly endowed 'agricultural bank.'   India has made a beginning full of promise.   And even in far Japan, and in China, people are trying to acclimatize the more perfected organizations of Schulze-Delitzsch and Raffeisen.   The entire world seems girdled with a ring of coöperative credit. Only the United States and Great Britain still lag lamentably behind."

BANKERS' SAVINGS BANKS

The saving banks of America present a striking contrast to these democratic banks.   Our savings banks also have performed a great service. They have provided for the people's funds safe depositories with some income return. Thereby they have encouraged thrift and have created, among other things, reserves for the proverbial "rainy day." They have also discouraged "old stocking" hoarding, which diverts the money of the country from the channels of trade. American savings banks are also, in a sense, banks *of* the people; for it is the people's money which is administered by them. The $4,500,000,000 deposits in 2,000 American savings banks belong to about ten million people, who have an average deposit of about $450. But our savings banks are not banks *by* the people, nor, in the full sense, *for* the people.

First: American savings banks are not managed *by* the people. The stock-savings banks, most prevalent in the Middle West and the South, are purely commercial enterprises, managed, of course, by the stockholders' representatives. The mutual savings banks, most prevalent in the Eastern states, have no stockholders; but the depositors have no voice in the management. The banks are managed by trustees *for* the people, practically a self-constituted and self-perpetuating body, composed of "leading" and, to a large

extent, public-spirited citizens. Among them
(at least in the larger cities) there is apt to be a
predominance of investment bankers, and bank
directors. Thus the three largest savings banks
of Boston (whose aggregate deposits exceed
those of the other 18 banks) have together 81
trustees. Of these, 52 are investment bankers or
directors in other Massachusetts banks or trust
companies.

Second: The funds of our savings banks
(whether stock or purely mutual) are not used
mainly *for* the people. The depositors are
allowed interest (usually from 3 to 4 per cent.).
In the mutual savings banks they receive ultimately all the net earnings. But the money
gathered in these reservoirs is not used to aid
productively persons of the classes who make
the deposits. The depositors are largely wage
earners, salaried people, or members of small
tradesmen's families. Statically the money is
used for them. Dynamically it is used for the
capitalist. For rare, indeed, are the instances
when savings banks moneys are loaned to advance productively one of the depositor class.
Such persons would seldom be able to provide
the required security; and it is doubtful whether
their small needs would, in any event, receive

consideration. In 1912 the largest of Boston's mutual savings banks—the Provident Institution for Savings, which is the pioneer mutual savings bank of America—managed $53,000,-000 of people's money. Nearly one-half of the resources ($24,262,072) was invested in bonds—state, municipal, railroad, railway and telephone and in bank stock; or was deposited in national banks or trust companies. Two-fifths of the resources ($20,764,770) were loaned on real estate mortgages; and the average amount of a loan was $52,569. One-seventh of the resources ($7,566,612) was loaned on personal security; and the average of each of these loans was $54,830. Obviously, the "small man" is not conspicuous among the borrowers; and these large-scale investments do not even serve the individual depositor especially well; for this bank pays its depositors a rate of interest lower than the average. Even our admirable Postal Savings Bank system serves productively mainly the capitalist. These postal saving stations are in effect catch-basins merely, which collect the people's money for distribution among the national banks.

PROGRESS

Alphonse Desjardins of Levis, Province of Quebec, has demonstrated that coöperative credit associations are applicable, also, to at least some urban communities. Levis, situated on the St. Lawrence opposite the City of Quebec, is a city of 8,000 inhabitants. Desjardins himself is a man of the people. Many years ago he became impressed with the fact that the people's savings were not utilized primarily to aid the people productively. There were then located in Levis branches of three ordinary banks of deposit—a mutual savings bank, the postal savings bank, and three incorporated "loaners"; but the people were not served. After much thinking, he chanced to read of the European rural banks. He proceeded to work out the idea for use in Levis; and in 1900 established there the first "credit-union." For seven years he watched carefully the operations of this little bank. The pioneer union had accumulated in that period $80,000 in resources. It had made 2900 loans to its members, aggregating $350,000; the loans averaging $120 in amount, and the interest rate 6 1/2 per cent. In all this time the bank had *not met with a single loss*. Then Desjardins·

concluded that democratic banking was applicable to Canada; and he proceeded to establish other credit-unions. In the last 5 years the number of credit-unions in the Province of Quebec has grown to 121; and 19 have been established in the Province of Ontario. Desjardins was not merely the pioneer. All the later credit-unions also have been established through his aid; and 24 applications are now in hand requesting like assistance from him. Year after year that aid has been given without pay by this public-spirited man of large family and small means, who lives as simply as the ordinary mechanic. And it is noteworthy that this rapidly extending system of coöperative credit-banks has been established in Canada wholely without government aid, Desjardins having given his services free, and his travelling expenses having been paid by those seeking his assistance.

In 1909, Massachusetts, under Desjardin's guidance, enacted a law for the incorporation of credit-unions. The first union established in Springfield, in 1910, was named after Herbert Myrick—a strong advocate of coöperative finance. Since then 25 other unions have been formed; and the names of the unions and of their officers disclose that 11 are Jewish, 8 French-Canadian, and 2 Italian—a strong indication that the immigrant is not unprepared for financial democracy. There is reason to believe that these people's banks will spread rapidly in the United States and that they will succeed. For the coöperative building and loan associations, managed by wage-earners and salary-earners, who joined together for systematic saving and ownership of houses—have prospered in many states. In Massachusetts, where they have existed for 35 years, their success has been notable—the number, in 1912, being 162, and their aggregate assets nearly $75,000,000.

Thus farmers, workingmen, and clerks are learning to use their little capital and their savings to help one another instead of turning over their money to the great bankers for safe keeping, and to be themselves exploited. And may we not expect that when the coöperative movement develops in America, merchants and manufacturers will learn from farmers and workingmen how to help themselves by helping one another, and thus join in attaining the New Freedom for all? When merchants and manufacturers learn this lesson, money kings will lose subjects, and swollen fortunes may shrink; but industries will flourish, because the faculties of men will be liberated and developed.

President Wilson has said wisely:

"No country can afford to have its prosperity originated by a small controlling class. The treasury of America does not lie in the brains of the small body of men now in control of the great enterprises. . . . It depends upon the inventions of unknown men, upon the originations of unknown men, upon the ambitions of unknown men. Every country is renewed out of the ranks of the unknown, not out of the ranks of the already famous and powerful in control."

THE END

Breinigsville, PA USA
23 March 2011
258254BV00003B/35/P